Palestinians in Israel

Segregation, Discrimination and Democracy

Ben White

Foreword by Haneen Zoabi

First published 2012 by Pluto Press
345 Archway Road, London N6 5AA

www.plutobooks.com

Distributed in the United States of America exclusively by
Palgrave Macmillan, a division of St. Martin's Press LLC,
175 Fifth Avenue, New York, NY 10010

British Library Cataloguing in Publication Data
A catalogue record for this book is available from the British Library

ISBN 978 0 7453 3229 1 Hardback
ISBN 978 0 7453 3228 4 Paperback

Library of Congress Cataloging in Publication Data applied for

10 9 8 7 6 5 4 3 2 1

Designed and produced for Pluto Press by Chase Publishing Services Ltd
Typeset from disk by Stanford DTP Services, Northampton, England
Simultaneously printed digitally by CPI Antony Rowe, Chippenham, UK and
Edwards Bros in the United States of America

To Ameer, Janan, Hind and Huda

From the window of my small cell
I can see trees smiling at me,
Rooftops filled with my people,
Windows weeping and praying
For me.
From the windows of my small cell
I can see your large cell.

Samih al-Qasim,
'End of a Discussion with a Jailer'

مِن كوّة زنزانتي الصُّغرى
أبصرُ أشجاراً تَبسمُ لي
وسطوحاً يملأها أهلي
ونوافذَ تبكي وتصلي
من أجلي
من كُوّةِ زنزانتي الصغرى
أبصرُ زنزانَتَكَ الكُبرى

سميح القاسم

Contents

List of Maps, Figures and Photographs

Maps

Figures

Photographs

Acknowledgements

As ever, there are too many people to thank and acknowledge, and I ask forgiveness from those I forget.

Firstly, I want to thank my wife Amanda for her patience with me as I wrote this. My work is for you and our two beautiful children, Isabella and Daniel. Thank you also to my family for their love and support.

Secondly, thank you to Roger van Zwanenberg and everyone at Pluto Press for their encouragement and hard work.

Thank you to Paul, Nadia, and Asa, who gave of their time in order to give me invaluable feedback. A special thank you to Nadia, and the rest of the staff at Adalah, for their willingness to help and give advice.

Thank you to the following, who in different ways have helped, encouraged, shaped, and contributed to this project, knowingly or otherwise. In no particular order: MK Haneen Zoabi, Ahmad Barclay and Dena Qaddumi at arenaofspeculation.org, Malkit Shoshan, Matan Cohen, Ilan Pappe, Isabelle Humphries, Oren Yiftachel, Chris Toensing at Middle East Report, Hanan Chehata at Middle East Monitor, Rev. Garth Hewitt and the Amos Trust staff, Orna Kohn, Suhad Bishara, Sawsan Zaher, Gaby Rubin, Jonathan Cook, Hassan Jabareen, Badil, Mohammad Zeidan at HRA, Sliman Abu-Abaid and Yeela Raanan at the Regional Council for the Unrecognised Villages of the Negev, Esam and family, Bassam, Riya al-Sanah, Hind Awwad, Mansour Nsasra, Rebecca Vilkomerson at JVP, Andy Slaughter MP, John McDonnell MP, Karma Nabulsi, As'ad Abu Khalil, Ali Abunimah, Yonatan Shapira, Omar Barghouti, Sami Awad and Holy Land Trust, William Dalrymple, Max Blumenthal, Ahdaf Soueif.

Finally, I would like to express gratitude, admiration, and love, to all those campaigners and activists – particularly students – I have met, collaborated with, and enjoyed time with, in the UK, Canada, and USA. Your energy, passion, and clarity of vision has always inspired and refreshed me.

Foreword

Haneen Zoabi

In seven chapters of penetrating analysis, author Ben White asks for a shift away from the paradigm of Occupation as the lens through which the Israeli-Palestinian conflict is viewed. For White, such a shift entails a dramatic transformation in the political assumptions and axioms that have prevailed in the post-Oslo era and, more importantly, a return to the historical and moral roots of the Palestinian question.

The argument that the relationship between Israel and the Palestinians is one of a conflict with a racist settler project that was founded on notions of ethnic purity is understood implicitly by all Palestinians. We Palestinians were quick to comprehend the relationship between ourselves – as indigenous inhabitants of this land – and those who came to take our place (in every sense) without even considering a common life with or alongside us, and without acknowledging that which had gone before them.

The core issue is not a shift in paradigm so much as a return to an old paradigm, that which dominated the Palestinian national liberation movement at least ten years prior to Oslo. I am a member of the political party that has revived this 'new/old' paradigm, as a part of a larger Palestinian political project. The focus of this project moved from the Diaspora – previously the heart of the Palestinian national movement – to the West Bank and Gaza Strip following the First Intifada, before shifting once again to rest on a group that had been regarded as marginal to, or even outside, the Palestinian national movement: the Palestinians whom Israel didn't expel in 1948.

The Oslo Accords were the culmination of a gradual process of decline within the Palestinian national project that began with the expulsion of the Palestinian Liberation Organisation (PLO) from Lebanon in 1982, and were accompanied by a re-writing of history and redefinition of the Palestinian question. Before

Oslo, the Palestinian issue was about the national liberation of the Palestinian people living in the Diaspora and in its homeland (in the 1948 and 1967 territories). It proposed a democratic solution for both Palestinians and Jews (and hence it also sought to liberate the Jews in Palestine from the racist project of which they are part).

Post-Oslo, the Palestinian question concentrated on the establishment of a state in the Palestinian territories occupied in 1967, and left intact the Jewish state that was constructed on the Palestinian territories occupied in 1948 and contains part of the Palestinian people. It was the result of the marriage of moderate Zionism and the lowest level of Palestinian aspirations, and according to the Oslo vision, there are no victims, no perpetrators and no acknowledgement of the legitimacy of resistance to the Occupation. It fails to view the Occupation from the perspective of values – that is, as an egregious violation of humanity and dignity that both calls for and legitimises resistance.

However, Oslo also produced its own antithesis, in the form of a political project that was to redefine the Palestinian issue – again – as one of confrontation with the Zionist project (which did not begin in 1967 and does not only concern the territories occupied in 1967 but the entire Palestinian people, and even the wider Arab region). Significantly, Oslo produced this antithetical project within the very group that it excluded: the Palestinians in Israel.

'The paradigm of Occupation' approached the Palestinians inside Israel as an internal Israeli matter. In response, this segment of the Palestinian people reformulated their national project in a manner that was to secure their reintegration into the Palestinian people and guarantee their place as an integral part of the Palestinian issue, both as part of the conflict and as part of the solution.

The Palestinians in Israel have been able to achieve this turnabout only by reinventing the confrontation with the Zionist project, of which they are a direct – and historically the oldest – outcome. Ironically, it was their Israeli citizenship that enabled them to do so. The Palestinians in Israel have successfully employed the contradiction between Zionism and democratic citizenship that was imposed on them to reconstruct their national project.

At a time when it appeared that the Palestinian national movement (the PLO) was abandoning the Palestinian liberation project, it was these Palestinians, citizens of Israel, who picked up the baton. After 50 years of political experiment in the context of our Israeli citizenship, the Palestinians in Israel have grasped the power that is inherent in the complicated demand for what is referred to as 'democracy', or full equality among citizens, part of whom belong to the 'expelled' people. These taken for granted demands, for the indigenous people and for 'full citizenship', are suffice to undermine the moral and political legitimacy of the entire Zionist project, and to relegate it to the status of a racist, colonialist venture.

The demand for a 'state of all its citizens' has put the Palestinians in Israel at the heart of the direct confrontation with the political rubric of 'the Jewish state' that epitomises the Zionist enterprise. The 'state of all its citizens' project has forced the 'Jewish state' to admit the primacy that it grants to Jewish-Zionist values over democratic values, and to recognise the impossibility of coexistence between the two.

Netanyahu may declare that Israel is 'the only democracy in the Middle East' and announce that 'Israel's Arab citizens enjoy real democratic rights' to the rapturous applause of uninformed members of a foreign congress. However, what he says to our face is that, 'Israel is a Jewish state', and there are now dozens of laws to prove it. We will not clap for him and he does not expect our applause.

After all, what is the recent 'legislation' pertaining to the Jewishness of the state, and the escalation of the process of Judaisation from the level of policy (see Chapter 3), if not a direct acknowledgment of the conflict between democracy and Zionism, and the privileging of the latter over the former?

This book's strength lies not only in its content, but also in its timing. Its release comes as a political culture that has proudly and tenaciously adopted elements of fascism reaches new heights. Israel has declared – with the sanction of the Attorney General – that it will target anyone who works against the Jewish identity of the state, even if he or she does so through legal means. It is a state that pursues repressive policies that are inconsistent with its own laws (as in Olmert's 2007 government) and then amends its laws to make them conform to its policy of political persecution (Netanyahu/Lieberman's 2010 government).

It is the essence of this fight that Ben White has traced out in a professional, profound, and moral manner, understanding that justice remains the primary lens through which to comprehend what has happened in Palestine and to advance our political platform.

August 2011

Map 1 Israel and its Palestinian population. (Map by Martin Brown Design, by kind permission of Yale University Press, appeared in Ilan Pappe's *The Forgotten Palestinians*)

Introduction

Our past lies before us
Our present inside us
Our future on our backs.
As though we were twenty impossibilities
In Lydda, Ramla and Galilee
O living roots hold fast
And – still – reach deep in the earth.

Tawfiq Zayyad (from 'Here We Shall Stay')[1]

IN FOCUS: THE PALESTINIAN CITIZENS OF ISRAEL

The description of Israel as 'the only democracy in the Middle East' has been received wisdom in the West for decades. The idea of Israel as 'one of us', a home for Western values in a region of religious extremism and political instability, is voiced and understood by politicians, journalists, analysts, and the general public. Even with the 2010–11 Arab uprisings across the region, as well as the supposedly 'democratizing' mission of the invasion and occupation of Iraq, the conception of Israel's status as regionally anomalous – a liberal, parliamentary democracy – remains unshaken. When President Barack Obama can call Israel a 'small nation' in a 'tough neighbourhood', remarkably little has changed since Theodor Herzl, the father of political Zionism, wrote in 1896 that a Jewish state in Palestine would be 'an outpost of civilization against barbarism'.[2]

More recently, Israeli policies have been subject to increased criticism, particularly in Europe. When these serious misgivings are expressed by mainstream Western politicians, the focus is on Israeli actions in the West Bank and Gaza Strip, the territories occupied since 1967. Some argue that Israel is understandably struggling to marry its commitment to democratic principles and the need to ensure security for its people.

Another, stronger critique has gained traction in some quarters that condemns Israel's military rule and colonization of the Occupied Palestinian Territories (OPT) in terms of apartheid and through the prism of the settlement enterprise. Whether criticising 'disproportionate' military action, or highlighting the radical Jewish settler movement, Western disapproval of Israeli policies is shaped by the assumption that it is the West Bank and Gaza where a Palestinian state will be created, and where Israeli settlement is unwise or illegitimate.

In the context of the official 'peace process', Israeli leaders – and in particular, Prime Minister Benjamin Netanyahu – have stressed the need for Palestinians to 'recognise' Israel as a 'Jewish state'. While this has been seen as a blocking tactic, there is more going on here: it reflects a profound crisis in the Israeli body politic – and at the centre of the storm is the 20 per cent of the country's citizens who are Palestinian. In parallel with the peace process floundering to the point of seeming irreversible failure, the Palestinian minority inside Israel is being increasingly targeted by the Israeli security-political establishment.

Yet despite the fact that the experience of Israel's second-class citizens is central to understanding the core of the conflict, their struggle is poorly understood, and ignored by the official peace process. Indeed, even to speak of the Palestinian citizens as such risks confusion, given that for so long, they have been referred to as 'Israeli Arabs' or the 'Arabs in Israel'. This is a deliberate formulation; as Professor Hillel Cohen has noted, 'creating this new Israeli Arab identity [has been] one of the state's tacit goals'.[3]

'Israeli Arabs' are the Palestinians and their descendents who were not expelled and denationalised with the establishment of Israel in 1948. Despite decades of coercion and control (including a generation of martial law), many of these Palestinian citizens are more determined than ever to challenge the structural discrimination and racist legislation which shapes their lives in the 'Jewish and democratic' state. While the 'Land Day' protests against land confiscation in 1976 was a seminal event, in more recent times the October 2000 protests and killings by security forces have come to shape significantly the relationship between the state and the minority.

Viewing Palestinian citizens as a threat is not just a response to an assertive politics of resistance from the minority: it is also a reflection of developments related to the peace process and the colonization of the OPT:

> By the end of the 1990s, Israel had, to a large extent, reached the limit of possible significant expansion and colonisation in the Occupied Territories ... In other words, for the last decade, Israel has focused less on expansion, and more on the consolidation of the existing colonies, cementing (literally) the apartheid regime over Palestinians.[4]

Thus as the possibility for expansion exhausts itself, the gaze has turned inwards, to the internal colonialism of 'Judaising' the Galilee and Negev (see Chapter 3) – the unfinished war of 1948. In other words, as imprisoned community leader and activist Ameer Makhoul has put it, the recent escalation in the targeting of Palestinian citizens is not about giving the state 'more control and power'; it is, in fact, 'the Israeli crisis'.[5]

Since 2000, Israeli lawmakers have proposed and passed a host of aggressively nationalistic and discriminatory laws. One can argue the phenomenon began with the Fifteenth Knesset (the Israeli parliament), 1999–2002, which 'took an active past in redrawing the boundaries of Arab citizenship, enacting a number of discriminatory laws affecting the Palestinian citizens' political participation, right of expression, economic status, and even family life'.[6]

But this trend accelerated post-2008, under the Ehud Olmert-led government, and then even more markedly with Netanyahu's Likud/Yisrael Beiteinu-dominated Knesset. The book will cover these developments in more depth, but just in the first few months of the Netanyahu government, cabinet ministers had already proposed an initiative for replacing all Arab names on road signs with Jewish ones, called for a halt to Arabs 'spreading' in a region dominated by the Palestinian minority, and declared that Palestinian citizens will be forbidden from teaching the Nakba (the expulsions of 1948).[7]

Even with attention being paid to issues like home demolitions, 'unrecognised villages', and a politics of challenging 'disloyal' citizens, the Palestinians in Israel are still 'forgotten' compared to those in the West Bank, Gaza, and even the regional refugee camps. Yet it is through understanding Israel's policies towards the Palestinian minority that we can grasp what is fundamentally at stake in the conflict, as well as help change the current paradigm for a fresh vision of justice and peace for Jews and Palestinians.

DENYING DEMOCRACY

Before looking forward, however, we need to look back. The dual focus of this book – how Israel has related to the Palestinian minority and what a 'Jewish and democratic' state really means – is impossible to understand without seeing how denying democracy has been part of the Zionist colonisation of Palestine from the very beginning. For the pre-state Zionist movement and its supporters in key Western governments like Britain, the indigenous Palestinian Arabs were of less value than the Jews; the rights of the former, trumped by the aspirations of political Zionism.

This sheds light on the Zionist motif of Palestine being 'empty' – like World Zionist Organisation co-founder Max Nordau writing in 1902 how the Zionists 'desire to irrigate with their sweat and to till with their hands a country that is today a desert, until it again becomes the blooming garden it once was'.[8] As Anton La Guardia put it, seeing the land as 'empty' was not a matter of ignorance of the Arab population but a question of 'European chauvinism':

> The 'invisibility' of the Arabs was self-serving. Palestine at the time of first Zionist settlement was not empty of people, but of people deemed worthy by Europeans of controlling their own country.[9]

The assumed inferiority of the Palestinians meant that their wishes were to be no obstacle to the realisation of the Zionist dream, a position not just embraced by the 'extremists'. Aaron

David Gordon, for example, an influential member of the Zionist labour movement, asked in 1921:

> And what did the Arabs produce in all the years they lived in the country? Such creations, or even the creation of the Bible alone, give us [Jews] a perpetual right over the land in which we were so creative, especially since the people that came after us ... did not create anything at all.[10]

Gordon, then, 'like all Zionists ... did not recognize the principle of majority rule'. Likewise, Israel's first Prime Minister, David Ben-Gurion, told the Peel Commission in 1937 that aside from the Jews, 'there is no other nation – I do not say population, I do not say sections of a people – there is no other race or nation as a whole which regards this country as their only homeland'.[11]

The intrinsic superiority of the Jewish claim to the land was a belief shared by a number of British politicians, including the former Secretary of State for the Colonies Winston Churchill, who, speaking at the Peel Commission, said:

> I do not admit that the dog in the manger has the final right to the manger, even though he may have lain there for a very long time. I do not admit that right. I do not admit, for instance, that a great wrong has been done to the Red Indians of America, or the black people of Australia. I do not admit that a wrong has been done to those people by the fact that a stronger race, a higher grade race, or, at any rate, a more worldly-wise race, to put it that way, has come in and taken their place.[12]

British Foreign Secretary Arthur Balfour, the author of the 1917 declaration, wrote in a memo to Lord Curzon that 'Zionism, be it right or wrong, good or bad, is rooted in age-long tradition, in present needs, in future hopes, of far profounder import than the desires and prejudices of the 700,000 Arabs who now inhabit that ancient land'.[13] It is unsurprising – though no less shocking – that Israel's first president Chaim Weizmann told Jewish Agency official Arthur Ruppin in 1936 that 'the British told us that there are some hundred thousand negroes [in Palestine] and for those there is no value'.[14]

The logical outcome of believing in the natives' inferiority was resistance to the application of democracy, and so both the Zionist leadership and their Western allies explicitly opposed the implementation of self-determination in Palestine. When, in 1935, the High Commissioner for the British Mandate proposed the establishment of a Legislative Council, the Zionists 'attack[ed] the project' because the Jews were 'to be allotted seats in proportion to their actual population'.[15] Much earlier, in 1919, the Zionist Organisation in London had warned that the problem with democracy is that it 'too commonly means majority rule without regard to diversities of types or stages of civilization or differences of quality'.[16]

Not all Western decision-makers went along with this disregard for Palestinian rights. After the UN vote to partition Palestine, the director of the US State Department's Office of Near Eastern and African Affairs, Loy Henderson, described the proposals to the Secretary of State George C. Marshall as 'in definite contravention of ... principles on which American concepts of government are based'. He continued:

> These proposals, for instance, ignore such principles as self-determination and majority rule. They recognize the principle of a theocratic racial state and even go so far in several instances as to discriminate on grounds of religion and race against persons outside of Palestine.[17]

SUMMARY

Establishing a Jewish state in Palestine was finally realised through the ethnic cleansing of up to 90 per cent of the Palestinians who would have lived inside the new borders.[18] But the opposition to Palestinian self-determination that expressed itself in the Mandate period continues right through to today. It is manifest in the angry response when Palestinian citizens propose that Israel should be a state for all, not some, of its citizens. It is there in the unabashed belief of Israeli leaders that only Jews have rights *to* the 'Land of Israel', while 'Arabs' may enjoy (conditional) rights *in* the land. Finally, it is expressed in

Israel's long-standing policies which ensure that Palestinians under the state's control, whether citizens or militarily occupied, are subject to control and segregation.

From the very beginning, the political Zionism project in Palestine has been, necessarily, anti-democratic and exclusivist. The Palestinian presence, at best, is 'tolerated' as a controlled minority that accepts Jewish sovereignty. Israel's policies towards Palestinians are shaped by the same priorities and assumptions in the hills of the West Bank as they are in the Galilee. In this book, I will look at what it means to be a Palestinian citizen in Israel, how that relates to the bigger questions, and argue that Israel's definition as 'Jewish and democratic' is the contradiction at the heart of the conflict.

1
'Jewish *and* Democratic'?

All Israeli citizens know that Israel has been, and must be, the most anti-racist state in the world.[1]

Israeli President Shimon Peres

A credible analysis of the Israeli regime ... cannot conclude that Israel is a democracy.[2]

Professor Oren Yiftachel, Ben-Gurion University

It has become commonplace to hear Israeli leaders and diplomats demand that the Palestinians 'recognise' Israel as a Jewish, or sometimes 'Jewish and democratic', state. In the context of the post-Oslo peace talks, this is a relatively recent addition. Indeed, before 2000, the topic of Israel's supposedly 'Jewish and democratic' character was not often reported on or discussed. Looking back through the news archives of the 1970s–90s, concern about preserving Israel as a 'Jewish and democratic' state was primarily part of a debate about the fate of the Palestinian territories occupied by Israel since in 1967.

Now, however, Israel's self-defined Jewish character is not only part of the peace process, but according to a number of Knesset lawmakers, it also needs 'defending'. For Israel's lobbyists and supporters internationally, opposition to Israel as a Jewish state is what makes so-called 'delegitimisation' so problematic. Therefore, it is vital to unpack the 'Jewish and democratic' formulation, particularly since understanding the significance of this self-definition also brings us closer to seeing the root cause of the conflict.

Firstly, in the words of Israeli academic Dr Haim Misgav, 'the State of Israel is not like other states', and this is distinctiveness openly celebrated.[3] Here, for example, is academic Eliezer Schweid, writing for the World Zionist Organization in 1970:

> As a Zionist State, the State of Israel, contrary to other states, must regard itself as the State of a people the majority of which is not concentrated within its borders. As a Zionist State, it must bear the responsibility for the security, well-being, unity and continuous cultural identity of the Jewish people ... [4]

Yet recall that one in five Israeli citizens are Palestinians. Thus, while Israel's 'frontier' extends to include 'every Jew, anywhere in the world', all of whom are considered potential citizens, 'at the same time, it remains a state for some, not all, of its actual citizens'.[5]

Secondly, when it comes to the crunch, one half of the 'Jewish and democratic' character carries more weight. Noam Arnon, a key personality in the settler movement, put it like this:

> By definition the state of Israel was founded as a Jewish state. The regime constituted in it is democratic in character, but its essence is Jewish. And if there is a contradiction between this essence and the character of the government, it is clear that the essence takes precedence ... [6]

This is not just the view of the political Right in Israel; as we will see, it is an understanding that shapes the legal, legislative, and bureaucratic spheres. It is a state 'created by and for Jews', and thus one that 'identifies with the core national group, rather than with its citizens as such'.[7]

Thirdly, the discrimination faced by the Palestinian minority that is inherent in the definition of Israel as 'Jewish and democratic' is readily acknowledged when the question is discussed honestly. Renowned jurist Ruth Gavison was once considered for a position on Israel's Supreme Court and was a founding member of the Association for Civil Rights in Israel. In 2003, Gavison wrote an extended defense of 'The Jews' right to statehood', and in doing so, was frank about the consequences for the Palestinians:

> The Jewish state is thus an enterprise in which the Arabs are not equal partners, in which their interests are placed below those of a different national group – most of whose members are newcomers to the land, and many of whom are not even living in the country.[8]

Likewise, in their study 'Civil religion in Israel', Israeli scholars Charles S. Liebman and Eliezer Don-Yeihya write that the 'very nature of [Israel's] civil religion excludes the Arabs' who are now around 20 per cent of the population.[9]

TWO LAWS FOR TWO PEOPLES

Foundational to how Israel as a Jewish state has worked out in practice for the Palestinian minority is legislation passed by the Knesset in 1950, namely the Absentee Property Law and the Law of Return. The implications of the former will be covered in more detail in Chapter 2, but for now it is instructive to hold up these two laws, passed in the same year, and see how together they defined 'the boundaries of exclusion ... and inclusion'.[10]

According to the Jewish Agency, the 'remarkable' Law of Return begins 'with a few simple words that defined Israel's central purpose: 'Every Jew has the right to immigrate to this country".[11] This meant that 'since then, Jews have been entitled to simply show up and declare themselves to be Israeli citizens ... Essentially, all Jews everywhere are Israeli citizens by right'.

Ben-Gurion noted that the Law of Return 'has nothing to do with immigration laws' in other countries, rooted in the 'historical right' of Jews to return from 'exile' to the 'fatherland'.[12] As Israeli journalist Anshel Pfeffer put it, the Law of Return is one of Israel's 'most fundamental documents', defining 'the nation's raison d'etre'.[13]

The Law of Return was later consolidated by the Citizenship Law of 1952, which granted citizenship to Jews who 'returned' (i.e. emigrated to Israel).[14] The Citizenship Law was also a legal cornerstone of Israel's ethnic cleansing of Palestine by, at a stroke, denationalising the hundreds of thousands of Palestinian refugees residing in camps over the border. This was achieved through the definition of 'Residency', a category intended to cater for the non-Jews in Israel. Yet a person only qualified if they were present for a registration survey in 1952 and had been so since the establishment of the state in May 1948. In other words, the over 700,000 Palestinians expelled by Israel and violently prevented from returning were deliberately excluded.

Such a policy went against United Nations General Assembly Resolution 181 (the Partition plan), which stipulated that residents of Mandate Palestine would 'become citizens of the State in which they are resident and enjoy full civil and political rights'.[15] It is also counter to Article 13 of the Universal Declaration of Human Rights which states that 'everyone has the right to leave any country, including his own, and to return to his country', and Article 15, which affirms that 'no one shall be arbitrarily deprived of his nationality'.[16] This is the key point: the ethnic cleansing of the Palestinian catastrophe, the Nakba, is what enabled a Jewish majority to be created at all. The context for even speaking of the 'Palestinian minority' in Israel is that they were, until 1948, the majority – and that today, in all of Palestine/ Israel, Palestinians are at least on parity with the number of Jews.

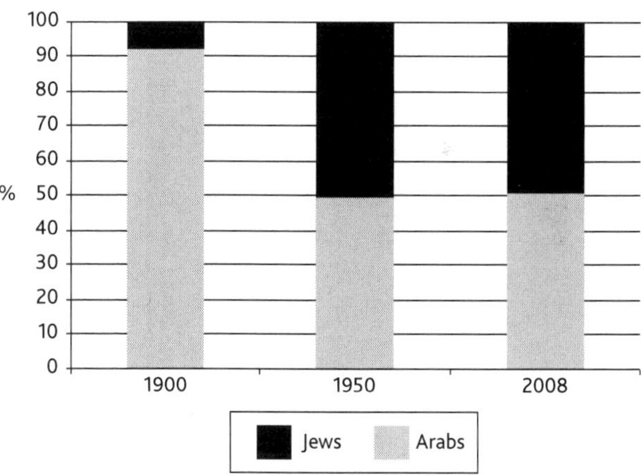

Figure 1 Demographics in Palestine/Israel (Mandate Palestine). (Source: Malkit Shoshan, *Atlas of the Conflict – Israel-Palestine*, pp. 170–71)

SPOT THE DIFFERENCE

A poorly understood aspect of Israel as a Jewish state is the distinction between 'citizenship' and 'nationality', an issue confused by the fact that in English the two terms can often be used interchangeably. In Israel, '"nationality" (Hebrew: 'le'um') and "citizenship" (Hebrew: "ezrahut") are two separate, distinct statuses, conveying different rights and responsibilities'.[17] Palestinians in Israel, as non-Jews, can be citizens, but never nationals, and are thus denied 'rights and privileges' enjoyed by those 'who would qualify for Israeli citizenship under the 1950 Law of Return'.[18]

Professor David Kretzmer, law scholar at Hebrew University and member of the International Commission of Jurists, has explained how this concept of 'nation' helps maintain 'the distinction between citizens of the state who belong to the Jewish people and those who do not ... [and] strengthens the dichotomy between the state as the political framework for all its citizens and the state as the particularistic nation-state of the Jewish people'.[19] International human rights expert Miloon Kothari, who served as UN Special Rapporteur on adequate housing for eight years, summed it up thus:

> Nationality status in Israel is not linked to origin from, or residence in a territory, as is the norm in international law. Rather, the basic theocratic character of the Israeli legal system establishes ethnic criteria as the grounds for the enjoyment of full rights. The Israeli Citizenship Law (ezrahut), officially mistranslated as 'Nationality Law', establishes a civil status distinct from 'Jewish nationality'.[20]

The difference between 'citizenship' and 'nationality' has been affirmed by Israeli courts. One such example is related by Bernard Avishai, in his book *The Hebrew Republic*, when in the early 1970s, a Jewish Israeli called George Tamarin petitioned the High Court to change the official registration of his nationality from Jewish to Israeli. Avishai records the High Court's ruling: that 'there is no Israeli nation separate from the Jewish nation', an assessment complemented by the then-president of the High Court Shimon Agranat, who said that a uniform Israeli nationality 'would negate the very foundation upon which the State of Israel was formed'.[21] In 2008, a group of petitioners again unsuccessfully requested for their nationality to be marked 'Israeli', claiming, 'that it made no sense for them to be Jews "for internal consumption" and Israelis "for external consumption"'.[22]

LET NO MAN PUT ASUNDER

While this use of 'nationality' as a means of privileging Jewish citizens at the expense of Palestinians is long-standing in Israel, in recent times there has been a further assault on the minority's citizenship rights. In 2003, the 'temporary' Nationality and Entry into Israel Law was passed by the Knesset, and at the time of writing, has been renewed ever since.[23] This law 'prohibits the granting of any residency or citizenship status to Palestinians from the 1967 Occupied Palestinian Territories (OPTs) who are married to Israeli citizens' (amended in 2007 to include citizens of 'enemy states' Iran, Iraq, Syria and Lebanon).

In a press release at the time, the Head of the Delegation of the European Commission to the State of Israel described the law as establishing 'a discriminatory regime to the detriment of Palestinians in the highly sensitive area of family rights'.[24] In 2008, Adalah, the Legal Centre for Arab Minority Rights in Israel, commented: 'It should be emphasized that no other state in the world denies the right to conduct a family life on the basis of national or ethnic belonging.'[25]

The public justification for this law was that it aimed to prevent Palestinians using 'family unification' as a means of gaining entry to Israel and committing terrorist attacks. Yet the 'security' rationale was flimsy: as the Legal Advisor to the Association for Civil Rights in Israel (ACRI) pointed out, Israel's security services had 'previously approved the entry of 20,000 Palestinian workers into Israel', showing it was entirely possible to 'assess the extent of the "danger" posed by Palestinian residents'.[26]

But the 'security' excuse is further undermined by remarks made by Israeli officials themselves, such as Gideon Ezra, then minister without portfolio and ex-deputy head of the Shin Bet, who affirmed that 'the state of Israel is not prepared to accept a creeping right of return; no one wants our state to cease to be a Jewish state'.[27]

In April 2005, the Israeli press reported that the government was 'planning legislative amendments that will make it more difficult for non-Jews to receive Israeli citizenship or permanent-resident status in Israel', a move 'aimed against granting legal status to Palestinians and other foreigners who have married Israeli citizens'.[28]

This legislation – 'based on the demographic consideration of ensuring a solid Jewish majority' – was linked in the reports to the 2003 'temporary' measure, and quoted then Prime Minister Ariel Sharon as unashamedly admitting: 'There is no need to hide behind security arguments. There is a need for the existence of a Jewish state.'[29]

Ha'aretz observed that there is 'broad agreement in the government and academia' that any such policies 'must be strict and make it difficult for non-Jews to obtain citizenship in Israel'.[30] Finally, this was also part of the context for the successfully-passed 'loyalty oath' initiative, which obliges non-Jewish candidates for citizenship to swear loyalty to a Jewish state. In July 2010, a government source said 'the wording of the declaration was designed to make it more difficult for Palestinians married to Israeli Arabs to gain citizenship on the basis of family unification'.[31]

ISRAEL'S 'CONSTITUTION'

Israel has no formal constitution. Of course, it is not alone in this respect, though its absence flies in the face of the UN Partition Plan, which required each state draft a 'democratic constitution ... guaranteeing all persons equal and non-discriminatory rights'.[32] But more problematic for the state's Palestinian minority than the absence of an actual constitution is what has developed in its place: a weakly-defined commitment to equality with elements of theocracy.

Over the years, Israel has passed eleven 'Basic Laws' which are the closest the state has to a legally-binding constitution. One of them, Basic Law: Human Dignity and Liberty (passed in 1992), appears on the surface to offer protection for all Israeli citizens, but in reality, the text is quite troubling for the Palestinian minority. Section 8 reads thus: 'There shall be no violation of rights under this Basic Law *except by a law befitting the values of the State of Israel*, enacted for a proper purpose, and to an extent no greater than is required [my emphasis]'.[33]

What are these 'values'? The Basic Law: Human Dignity and Liberty begins: 'The purpose of this Basic Law is to protect human dignity and liberty, in order to establish in a Basic Law the values of the State of Israel *as a Jewish and democratic state* ... [my emphasis]'.

In other words, there is 'a basis for giving significant weight to the nature of Israel as a Jewish state and its goals, at the expense of the fundamental rights concerned'.[34] As Supreme Court Judge Barak put it, when commenting on this interpretation: 'Israel is different from other countries. It is not only a democratic State, but also a Jewish State'.[35]

Revealingly, 'in spite of a number of attempts to present a bill of rights to the Knesset, no such bill has been enacted'.[36] Thus while there are affirmations of the principle of equality in rulings of the Supreme Court and in different legislation, there are profound 'limitations'.[37] This problem is shown in the addition of Section 7A in 1985 to Basic Law: The Knesset, which bans electoral candidates if they deny 'the existence of the State of Israel as the state of the Jewish people'. Naturally, the same amendment also prohibits denying 'the democratic nature of the state'.[38]

Israel also continues to be in an official 'state of emergency', which the Knesset has annually renewed since 1948. There are still 11 laws and 58 ordinances that depend on the state of emergency, covering a wide range of matters.[39]

> These include, for example, laws upholding emergency regulations regarding travelling abroad, the law to prevent infiltration, the law enabling the army to commandeer private property, the seafaring vessels law, the emergency laws for arrests, searches and land confiscation, the law supervising goods and services and the law prohibiting baking at night.[40]

Despite calls for the abolition of the state of emergency, these powers persist partly because to replace the powers granted to the Israeli government 'would require the establishment of arrangements that infringe on human rights'.[41]

Since 1948, Israel has also incorporated elements of theocracy into everyday life. This has meant 'governmental and legal discrimination' for Palestinian citizens, as well as non-Orthodox Jews, as these extracts from the US State Department's 'International Religious Freedom Report 2010' show.[42]

- The only in-country Jewish marriages the government recognizes are those performed by the Orthodox chief rabbinate.
- The rabbinate determines who is buried in Jewish state cemeteries, limiting this right to individuals considered Jewish by Orthodox standards.
- The government funded the construction of Jewish synagogues and cemeteries. The state contributes to the maintenance of non-Jewish places of worship, at a disproportionately lower level than for synagogues. In some areas the government allowed private citizens or municipalities to turn old mosques into galleries, restaurants, and museums.
- The Ministry of Religious Affairs has jurisdiction over the country's 133 Jewish religious councils, which oversee the provision of religious services for Jewish communities. A single non-Jewish religious council exists for the Druze and is overseen by the MOI's Department of Non-Jewish Affairs.
- The 2009 budget for religious services and religious institutions for the Jewish population was approximately $390 million. Religious minorities, which constituted

slightly more than 20 percent of the population, received approximately $14.2 million, or less than 4 percent of total funding.
- Numerous tourists were temporarily detained for religious reasons at Ben-Gurion Airport, prevented from entering Israel, and sent back to their source countries because of the MOI's 'suspicions of missionary activity'.

Some will point to Israel's Declaration of Independence, and its promise of 'complete equality of social and political rights to all [the country's] inhabitants', in an attempt to argue that minority rights are adequately protected. However, as Kretzmer points out, Israel's Supreme Court has not considered the Declaration a 'constitutional law' that can determine 'the validity or invalidity of ordinances and statutes'.[43] In fact, the state proclaimed by the much-touted Declaration was 'not a state of all its citizens' or 'even a Jewish-democratic state', but rather, 'a Jewish state, pure and simple'.[44]

A MEANS TO AN END

A further dimension of how Israel has structured and protected its Jewish character has been the role of the Zionist institutions, the Jewish Agency and the World Zionist Organisation. These bodies, whose raison d'être is to benefit Jews, have been granted responsibilities normally performed by the state, through legislation that makes them 'integral elements of the governmental apparatus'.[45] The World Zionist Organisation/Jewish Agency (Status) Law of 1952 (amended in 1975) grants the JA and WZO the status of

> authorized agencies which will continue to operate in the State of Israel for the development and settlement of the country, the absorption of immigrants from the Diaspora and the coordination of the activities in Israel of Jewish institutions and organizations active in those fields ...[46]

The usefulness of these organisations from the point of view of maintaining – yet also concealing – a regime of ethno-religious privilege was recognised by Ben-Gurion, who said that the Zionist Organisation 'is able to achieve what is beyond the power and competence of the State, and that is [its] advantage'.[47] Ben-Gurion expounded a similar argument in other contexts: in 1967, referring to the establishment of the Council for Demography (see Chapter 3), he said that the 'encouragement of [Jewish] childbearing' would 'have to be done on a voluntary basis by one or more Jewish bodies' that 'do not represent the state'.[48]

In his book *The Hebrew Republic*, Bernard Avishai cites the views of a former head of education at the Jewish Agency, who said that 'the only way to reconcile the existence' of such an organisation 'with the workings of a democratic state' was to 'reconfigure it as a huge NGO'.[49] All over the world, private organisations exist for the benefit of one particular group. But in Israel, bodies that are constitutionally obliged to privilege the interests of Jews are placed in positions of authority where they have the ability to prejudice the interests of non-Jewish citizens.

AN IRRESOLVABLE CONTRADICTION

In March 2011, prior to the Knesset passing the law on admissions committees (see Chapter 3), MK David Rotem responded to the legislation's critics by saying: 'I am not ashamed that I want to maintain this country as a Jewish and democratic state. You are worried about democracy, but in your way there would be no state. Israel is a Jewish and democratic state, not a state of all its citizens.'[50]

Rotem, who is from the Right of the Israeli political spectrum, does not see the contradiction in his logic, but nor do 'liberal-left' defenders of Israel's 'Jewish democracy'. The rest of this book details a variety of ways in which Israel's institutional discrimination works out in practice, but this should not come as a surprise. As Israeli professor Oren Yiftachel has put it, 'Israel's very regime structure makes equality between Arab and

Jew impossible in practice and in theory', since 'the state system is predicated on a constitutional arrangement that contradicts the conditions of equal citizenship, and, therefore, democracy'.[51] Critically, 'the essence of this contradiction stems from Israel's very raison d'être'.

In 2010, a controversy arose over a call from a number of rabbis in Israel for Jews to refrain from renting property to Arabs.[52] These are the kinds of comments that draw criticism from Israeli leaders, though just months later, a cabinet minister helped present a prize to one of the signatories, the rabbi of Safed, for his 'actions, effort and devotion to the Jewish nature of the Land of Israel'.[53] Yet singling out these rabbis for opprobrium is disingenuous. Writing in *Ha'aretz*, the founding chair of Ben-Gurion University's sociology and anthropology department Lev Luis Grinberg highlighted the hypocrisy:

> Like it or not, the fact is that the rabbis simply put into clear words the anti-democratic implications of the term 'Jewish State'. It is the privileges of Israel's Jewish citizens and the policy of progressively marginalizing the Arabs that are the source of racism. The rabbis are outspoken about it, the Knesset and government prefer a more subtle approach.[54]

Rather than a democracy, Yiftachel and others describe Israel as an 'ethnocracy', a regime that 'promote[s] the expansion of the dominant group in contested territory and its domination of power structures while maintaining a democratic facade'.[55] 'Despite declaring the regime as democratic, ethnicity (and not territorial citizenship) is the main determinant of the allocation of rights, powers, and resource ... [and] the logic of ethnic segregation is diffused into the social and political system.'[56]

A useful illustration of the significance of this for Palestinian citizens is the distinction made in a Knesset debate in 2002 by the then Prime Minister Ariel Sharon, who affirmed that Palestinian citizens had 'rights in the land' but 'all rights over the Land of Israel are Jewish rights'.[57] This was a point he repeated in the UN in 2005, when Sharon spoke of 'the right of the Jewish people *to* the Land of Israel', while 'others' only have rights '*in* the land' (my emphasis).[58] A similar insight was contained in a rare interview with religious Jewish settlers in the Sheikh Jarrah neighbourhood of Occupied East Jerusalem. Speaking to the *Jerusalem Post*, the husband elaborated on his position towards the 'Arabs':

> But in general – and this is my personal position – our attitude toward the Arabs is that I don't have any antagonism toward any Muhammad or Mustafa here; I don't have personal problems with them. It's a national issue here. We want to be in those specific places. It has to be clear that Eretz Yisrael in general and Jerusalem in particular belong to the Jewish people, and they have to understand that ... *The important point is that they have to admit who the landlord is here*. I don't mean regarding financial issues, like to whom you pay rent or that, but whom does this place belong to?[59] [My emphasis]

Honestly and pithily put, this is the point. Palestinian citizens, while 'formally enjoy[ing] civil and political rights' as individuals, experience an 'exclusion' effected by a dominant 'discourse of citizenship' whereby 'Jewish ethnicity is a necessary condition for membership of the political community'. With that exclusion assumed, Palestinian citizens can '[exercise] their individual rights, as long as these rights do not conflict with the national goals of the Jewish majority'.[60]

This explains the response in Israel when Palestinian citizens propose making Israel a state of all its citizens, like this example of an editorial in the *Jerusalem Post* in June 1976 that responded to a call from Arab mayors thus: 'It may ... be essential to reiterate to Israel's Arab citizens that while they have an inalienable right to fight for greater equality and more opportunities – a fight in which many Jews will enlist on their side – Israel is, and will remain, irrevocably Jewish.'[61]

Fast forward to the twenty-first century and little has changed. The same newspaper, reacting to calls from Palestinian civil society in Israel for a democratic state in 2007, condemned the call for a 'democratic, bilingual and multicultural' state as 'enticing and deceptive'.[62]

The tension in the 'Jewish and democratic' formulation is also shown by attitudes towards the Palestinian refugees. In his book *Sacred Landscape*, the former deputy mayor of Jerusalem, Meron Benvenisti, cites a 'prominent left-winger' unashamedly saying that he doesn't 'have any problem with the fact that we threw them [the Palestinians] out, and we don't want them back, because we want a Jewish state'.[63] In an article in the *Independent* in April 2011 on the fate of the still-standing village of Lifta, an official from the Israel Land Administration noted that 'if we waited for all the refugees to come back, we wouldn't have a country'.[64]

Before concluding this chapter, I want to return to the argumentation offered by Professor Ruth Gavison, whose essay 'The Jews' right to statehood: a defense' I cited earlier.[65] Acknowledging that Palestinians in the Jewish state are limited in 'their ability to ... exercise their right to self-determination', Gavison adds that 'this is far from being sufficient grounds' for making Israel a state of all its citizens. She justifies this by claiming that Palestinians only suffer 'limited harm', while by contrast, 'the Jewish people's rights' would suffer a 'mortal blow' if the state was genuinely democratic.

On the one hand, Gavison tries to infer that the Palestinian minority may simply 'not enjoy a feeling of full membership in the majority culture'. But on the other hand, Gavison can be more forthright about the full implications of Israel's Jewish character for the Palestinian minority: 'We must recognize that the needs of Jewish nationalism do, in some cases, justify certain restrictions on the Arab population in Israel, particularly in areas such as security, land distribution, population dispersal, and education.'

That is to say, clear, serious material discrimination is at stake. Moreover, at no point does Gavison acknowledge the fundamental act of dispossession of Palestinians which enabled the establishment of the state in the first place; an act, needless to say, of greater significance than uncomfortable 'feelings'. The full extent of these 'certain restrictions', namely official policies of segregation and a regime of ethno-religious privilege, are laid out in the following chapters.

2
The Land Regime

If we needed this land, we confiscated it from the Arabs. We had to create a Jewish state in this country, and we did.[1]

Israeli Prime Minister Menachem Begin's adviser on Arab affairs Benyamin Gur-Arye.

Israel's land regime is a tool for and an outcome of mass usurpation of Palestinian land.[2]

The defining dynamic between the state and the Palestinian minority has been the expropriation of, and alienation from, land. Legal scholars Hussein Abu Hussein and Fiona McKay have summarised the 'three main tools' in Israel's 'exclusionary land regime' as: (a) dispossession; (b) 'The regime for the ownership and administration of non-private land'; (c) 'The system regulating land development and land-use planning'.[3]

This chapter explores how these three tools have been employed historically, and how the modern day Israeli state maintains a discriminatory regime over that most basic element of individual and communal life – land.

LEGISLATING DISPOSSESSION

Between 1947–49, as Palestinians fled in fear and were pushed out of their homes and villages, the Israeli authorities' approach to 'abandoned' property was not always organised, and some seizure of homes and land took place on a somewhat ad hoc basis.[4] Reasonably quickly, however, the government acted to make the removal of over 700,000 Palestinians an 'on the ground' reality. After all, in June 1948 Israeli intelligence had described the potential 're-establishment [of the refugees] in the villages' as a threat to the 'achievements' of the war.[5] Thus the demolition of Palestinian villages that same month 'took on the character of a political mission whose objective was to block the return of the refugees to their homes'.[6]

Many Jewish immigrants were directly resettled in empty Palestinian homes, most often in the cities, but also in rural communities that were not leveled by the Israeli military. Around 45,000 immigrants were settled in Palestinian homes in Jaffa, around 40,000 in downtown Haifa and about 5,000 in Acre.[7] Some of these Jewish Israelis expressed their unease at being in recently 'abandoned' homes, such as the following member of Sasa kibbutz, built on the ethnically cleansed village of Sa'sa':

> Living in an Arab village, in homes of people who had left in an awful hurry, a short time before we arrived. [...] Here we were, American Jewish pioneers, come to help build a new homeland and create a new society [...] ... It was bad enough living in the village were you could almost feel their presence, where part of their possessions were left behind, with their store rooms filled with last seasons' crop. [...] If all this wasn't enough to destroy our ideological balloon, there was a problem of what to do with the mosque [...].[8]

But there was never any doubt that the sheer scale of the land and property belonging to expelled Palestinians was going to require a comprehensive legal solution. At the end of November 1947 there were 279 Jewish settlements in Mandate Palestine: by the end of August 1949, this had increased by 50 per cent, with most 'established on Arab-owned land'.[9] The statistics show the extent to which the new Jewish state was built on the ruins of a shattered Palestinian society:

In mid 1949, two-thirds of all land sown with grain was abandoned Arab land.[10]

By 1950, cooperative settlements held 45 per cent of abandoned or confiscated Palestinian land.[11]

95 per cent of new Jewish settlements established 1948–53 were on absentee property.[12]

In 1954, more than one third of Israel's Jewish population lived on absentee property.[13]
In 1951, abandoned land accounted for nearly 95 per cent of all Israel's olive groves and almost 10,000 acres of vineyards.[14]

The passing of the Absentee Property Law in 1950 was foundational to the development of an exclusionary land regime, the beginning of 'a complex mechanism of expropriation' to realise the 'permanent alienation of [Palestinian absentee] land in favour of the Jewish State'.[15] The government, however, was keen to obscure this reality: 'When the Minster of Finance brought the Absentees' Properties Law before the Knesset he warned the members not to talk carelessly: 'We are a small country,' he said, 'but the interest of the world in all that happens and is said here is immense'.[16] A lot of information regarding the government's policy towards abandoned property was kept secret: 'sessions of the Knesset's Finance Committee, when it discussed the problem, were closed'.[17]

The Law placed all property belonging to the Palestinian refugees in the hands of a Custodian of Absentee Property. Naturally, 'the most important provision in the statute is the definition of the term "absentees' property"', and 'it is in this very provision that the "catch" in the statute lies'.[18] While excluding Jewish Israelis from its provisions, the wording of the Law stripped Palestinian refugees – including internally displaced citizens (the 'present absentees') – of their property. 'Anyone who simply went on a business trip or family visit to neighbouring countries in the months between November 1947 and May 1948 was an absentee.'[19]

The result was that 'in urban areas the Custodian became Israel's largest landlord', holding and renting more than 65,000 houses and business belonging to Palestinian refugees.[20] A government figure for rural land that was placed under the Custodian's authority is 3.25 million dunams (an area over double the size of Greater London).[21]

In 1953 the absentee property held by the Custodian was transferred to the Development Authority, a body also established in 1950.[22] This Authority in turn was able to sell land on to the state and the Jewish National Fund (JNF) (see later in this chapter). Commenting on the Development Authority Law, the chairman of the Jewish National Fund's Board of Directors described it as 'based upon a sort of legal fiction'. 'It was not desired to transfer abandoned land to government ownership, as this would be interpreted as confiscation of the abandoned property.'[23] A distinction no doubt lost on the Palestinian refugees.

Numerous other laws were used by the Israeli authorities to confiscate land. One example is the Emergency Land Requisition of 1949, which though giving the government the power to confiscate land in the case of 'emergency', by 1953 had been used for over 1,000 orders, 'half of them for the purposes of settling new immigrants'.[24] Other methods used depended on the military rule to which most Palestinian citizens were subjected after 1948, like Article 125 of the Emergency Regulations. This enabled an area to be declared 'closed' and then, using the Land Acquisition (Validation of Acts and Compensation) Law (1953), the Ministry of Agriculture could declare the land 'uncultivated' and expropriate it for Jewish use. Shimon Peres praised the use of Article 125 as a means of 'directly continu[ing] the struggle for Jewish settlement and Jewish immigration'.[25]

After the key legislation used to carry out this mass transfer of land ownership had been passed in the first half of the 1950s, attention turned to taking as much land as possible from the remaining Palestinian communities. Part of this new strategy meant sending out government inspectors 'to the Palestinian villages and towns to claim the land of those who could be defined as absentees on behalf of the Custodian'.[26] There was a general drive to settle land title in the Galilee, 'in an attempt to prevent Arabs from acquiring property rights to these lands'.[27] As the head of the Registration and Settlement Department put it in 1959, the work was being done 'especially for clarifying the prospects of [Jewish] settlement in areas that are mainly inhabited by Arabs, mostly on land claimed by the State'.[28] Yosef Weitz, then head of JNF's Land Department and member of a committee for 'Land Settlement' in the Galilee, said in 1957 that the 'goal of the work' was first, 'to establish the ownership of the State on its land', and second, 'the Judaization of the Galilee'.[29]

Thus when it came to Palestinian land ownership claims, the Israeli government challenged 'everything it possibly could', meaning that 'sometimes it would hold tiny plots in the middle of village land'.[30] The existence of 'state land' within a village – 'a consequence of the seizure of refugee land' – meant a 'high degree of land fragmentation' in Palestinian communities.[31] Subsequently, the Israeli Land Administration (ILA) has 'offered' parcels of land taken from refugees back to their families, in exchange for agricultural land around the village. Even so, the ILA 'often maintains a 10–25 per cent ownership of the land parcel within the village' and thus 'continued control'.[32]

Through the 1950s, 1960s and 1970s, the Israeli state pursued Palestinian land for expropriation as vigorously as possible. Whether as refugees or citizens (or both), the odds were stacked against the Palestinians being able to hold on to their property. Hussein Abu Hussein and Fiona McKay have suggested that 'the figure of an average of at least 70 per cent of land lost to the Palestinian communities is plausible'.[33] Professor Ian Lustick, writing in 1980, estimated that between 65 and 75 per cent of the Palestinian citizens' land had been expropriated.[34]

The Israeli land regime was finally formalised in 1960, with the passing of Basic Law: Israel Lands in 1960. At the same time, the Israel Lands Administration (ILA) was established, centralising the administration of the state's land (including that held by the Jewish National Fund) in a single body. The ILA manages 93 per cent of all the land in Israel (for recent land reform, see later in this chapter). When Basic Law: Israel Lands was being presented to the Knesset, the then-Minister of Religious Affairs and Chair of the Constitution, Law and Justice Committee Zerah Wahrhaftig said:

> We want to make it clear that the land of Israel belongs to the people of Israel. The 'people of Israel' is a concept that is broader than that of the 'people resident in Zion' [i.e. Israel/Palestine], because the people of Israel live throughout the world.[35]

Finally, the legislative apparatus that enshrines the alienation of Palestinians from their land is still being added to and amended. A significant element of this is the 2009-enacted land reforms, to be discussed later in the chapter. But there have been other developments. The British Mandate-era Land (Acquisition for Public Purposes) Ordinance of 1943 has been used by the Israeli state to confiscate Palestinian land, without even the requirement of providing 'details of the nature of the public purpose for which the expropriation is required'.[36] In November 2010, an amendment was passed which 'confirms state ownership of land confiscated under this law, even where it has not been used to serve the original confiscation purpose'.

> The new law was designed to prevent Arab citizens from submitting lawsuits to reclaim confiscated land: over 25 years have passed since the confiscation of the vast majority of Palestinian land, and large tracts have been transferred to third parties, including Zionist institutions like the JNF.[37]

Photograph 1 Refugees from al-Birwa and Israelis on a Zochrot tour to the remains of the village, 2 July 2011. (Photograph taken by Fadi Kanaan)

MAKING THE DESERT BLOOM: 'DISAPPEARING' BEDOUIN PALESTINIANS

As part of the drive to dispossess the remaining Palestinians post-1948, the Israeli state took a particularly brutal approach to the Bedouins of al-Naqab, or the Negev. After the establishment of Israel (the Nakba), around 11,000 Bedouin Palestinians remained in the Negev, a mere 15–20 per cent of the population at the end of the British Mandate.[38]

The remaining Bedouin were eventually 'forcibly removed from their traditional lands and transferred into a reservation', a small area of the Negev that was called 'Siyag' (meaning 'fence' or 'enclosed area').[39] Not only was the Siyag 'about 10 per cent of the area formerly occupied exclusively by Bedouin', but there were already some tribes living there.[40] Conditions were harsh: under the military regime, 'no stone or concrete building activity was allowed', while 'throughout this period tribes were moved from one location to another', with 'some relocating up to five times in one year'.[41]

Israel has found it easy to manipulate a legal process of land expropriation in the Negev, owing to many Bedouin Palestinians' traditional approach to possession and ownership similar to other indigenous people groups around the world. Particularly relevant was the government's embrace of 'laws and regulations from the Ottoman legal system', which were employed in order to define Bedouin land as 'uncultivated and classified under state ownership'.[42]

In addition, the 1953 Real Estate Acquisition Law expropriated 'any land that was unsettled and uncultivated as of 1 April 1952'; meaning that 'since most of the Bedouin Arabs were forcibly evacuated from their land before this date, they lost their land rights even though they had ownership certificates'.[43] Professor Oren Yiftachel estimates that the pre-1948 community of the Negev 'lost more than 95 per cent of its landed property' through the different laws and bureaucratic processes Israel employed.[44]

Since 1948, dozens of Jewish communities have been established over land previously held by Bedouin Palestinians.

This parallel displacement and settlement echoes the words of JNF official Yosef Weitz, who in January 1948 said:

> The Hebrew state will have to embark on a wide settlement strategy in its first three years ... [a] big part of it in the Negev ... In the Negev we'll be able to implement immediately our development laws, according to which we shall expropriate land according to a well-designed plan.[45]

This dispossession continued through the decades, right up the present day. In the 1960s, an inter-ministerial committee was established to 'examine possible sites for residential construction in the Negev, including housing for the Bedouin population'.[46] The aim was to concentrate the Bedouin 'in a handful of townships inside the Siyag to free up land for Jewish settlement and army bases'.[47] In 1979, *Time* magazine reported on government plans 'to seize 37,500 acres of Bedouin land', forcing the population 'to resettle into new industrial townships'.[48] The article quoted one official as remarking: 'I'm not giving good Jewish land and water to Arabs'. The Israeli Prime Minister's 'adviser on Arab affairs' at the time, shrugged: 'They can double up in their tents until the villages are ready. They're used to it.'

Another tool in the hands of the state has been the so-called Green Patrol, a kind of paramilitary enforcement unit established in the late 1970s as an initiative of the Nature Reserves Authority, Jewish National Fund, Land Authority, and Ministry of Agriculture.[49] In 1977, the then Minister of Agriculture, Ariel Sharon, commented that he 'launched' the offensive 'to stem the hold of foreigners on state lands'.[50] During Sharon's time at the Ministry, the Green Patrol removed 900 Bedouin settlements and 'cut goat herds by more than ⅓'.[51] In a report on Green Patrol activities in 1981, the head of Israel's Nature Conservation Authority said that 'Bedouin life is finished'.[52] The Green Patrol still exists today.

At the time of writing, the Israeli government under Netanyahu is preparing to announce a new plan that is reported to involve the forced relocation of between 30,000 and 40,000 Bedouin and the expansion of existing townships.[53] Details were vague about how many of the unrecognised villages would be demolished or authorised. The context is a desire by the state to provide a more comprehensive 'solution' to the Bedouin issue, with reports also indicating that the state intends to dismiss half of all Bedouin land claims.[54]

The intention behind the desire to finalise the 'problem' of Bedouin land claims in the Negev is clear. In the case of one Bedouin community, documents are in the public realm that show how the land 'slated to be evicted under a proposed government plan will be used for the construction of a new Jewish community'.[55] As Negev council head Shmuel Rifman put it, 'If they don't finalize the Bedouin settlement it will be very hard to enhance Jewish settlement in the Negev. This must be addressed if one wants 700,000 Jews in the Negev.'[56]

Photograph 2 Khashm Zanna, Palestinian Bedouin unrecognised village, with the Israeli city Beersheva in the background. (January 2010, Ben White)

PRESENT ABSENTEES

The so-called 'present absentees' are Palestinians who were displaced from their homes in the Nakba, and though they remained in what became Israel, lost their property. They are, in a sense, internally displaced persons, though they are able to walk past the land or homes that were confiscated and transferred to state ownership. Their land was taken using the same mechanisms that stripped Palestinian refugees outside Israel of their property, even if they had only left their homes for a short time and, it is worth repeating, despite being citizens. In 1951, 'the sites of the abandoned villages were declared security areas, permitting legal measures against anyone entering them. This was an intermediary step toward turning them into Jewish villages.'[57]

Perhaps 'the most famous case of the internally displaced' was the (Christian) Palestinians of two villages, Kafr Bir'im and Iqrit.[58] The villagers were expelled by the Israeli military in 1948, though were told that the displacement would be 'temporary'. As the months became years, the Palestinians took their case to the courts. Yet while the case of Iqrit was still pending, Israeli forces blew up every house in the village. Kafr Bir'im, meanwhile, was declared a 'closed area' for security reasons, thus requiring a permit for entry: permits the army refused to give. In 1953, after the Finance Ministry had confiscated the land on the pretext that it was 'abandoned' and 'uncultivated' by the owners, the army destroyed the remaining houses. 'The lands of the villages were confiscated, declared "state lands", and leased to Jewish agricultural and urban settlements.'[59]

Many residents, however, refused to give up, mobilising international support and continuing different avenues of legal struggle. Despite offers of compensation and a government committee's proposal for a compromise deal, the reasoning behind the Israeli state's refusal to countenance a return of Palestinian citizens to their own land is instructive. In 2001, the security cabinet confirmed the decision to prevent a return to the two villages, 'keen to avoid setting a precedent' with regards to 'thousands of requests by displaced Arabs'.[60]

In 2003, the High Court accepted the government's argument, including an affidavit by the then Prime Minister Ariel Sharon, who said 'reasons of state' were involved. The government claimed that: 'accepting the petition would have far-reaching and strategic implications that would harm Israel's vital interests, because 200,000 other displaced citizens have also demanded they be allowed to return to their former villages.'[61]

Photograph 3 Nakba Day march 2008, Saffuriyya. (Ben White)

The Palestinians of Iqrit try and maintain their connection to the land, including summer day-camps for children and holding services in the still-standing church.[62] This kind of resistance to the state's policies is exemplified on a larger scale by the grassroots umbrella group, the Association for the Defence of the Rights of the Internally Displaced (ADRID). Organisers of the now annual march to commemorate the Nakba and demonstrate for the rights of the present absentees, ADRID was 'formed in order to campaign for the right of return for refugees inside Israel – as part of the development of the wider international grassroots campaign for the Palestinian right of return'.[63]

ADMINISTRATIVE APARTHEID

> 'State' ownership of land has a rather special meaning in a context where that 'state' is defined as the state of the Jewish people, rather than as the state of all its citizens.[64]

> More than 90 per cent of the land in Israel is state owned or controlled ... [a mechanism] designed to keep land in Jewish hands.[65]

As mentioned earlier, the formalisation of the Israeli land regime was primarily accomplished in 1960, with the passing of Basic Law: Israel Lands, and other associated legislation. By that time,

Ziad Awaisy

Ziad Awaisy was born in Nazareth in 1974, the son of refugees from Saffuriyya, just four miles away. The village was ethnically cleansed in 1948, with a pine forest planted on the site. A Jewish community was also established on the land (Tzippori).

'As a young child I always knew I was from Saffuriyya, I heard it all the time – "You are not from Nazareth" – Everybody said this. I remember my older cousins talking about it. I knew it before I knew what it meant.'

Ziad describes sitting with his grandmother and grandfather, whom he lived with, and listening to their stories ... 'I would absorb it from them, watch their movements as they were talking, follow their expressions'. Most painful to recall is his late grandmother whom he asked to accompany him to the land of Saffuriyya many times – 'And she would refuse saying, "If you take me back there you will have to leave me there".'

'When I grew up it wasn't enough just for me to feel what they [our grandparents] passed. I asked deeper questions about right and wrong, about power and weakness ... and to try and see other aspects of life from this perspective. I feel more committed to pass on what my grandfather had been through – they didn't pass it on as they should have because of the weight of the Nakba ... because they were just struggling to see that their sons and daughters lived. I feel my responsibility and role and this now is heavier than that of the second generation. The third generation feels it heavier; and the Israelis should know this.'

Source: Isabelle Humphries, 'Our Struggle is One and the Same', *Al Majdal*, Honoring the Struggle for Justice & Dignity (Winter 2007–Spring 2008)

the JNF had long since acquired large amounts of Palestinian land, having 'bought' around 40 per cent of abandoned property from the government.[66] The laws of the 1960s thus established a discriminatory system 'for the administration of public land' by giving 'a body that acts in the interests of one category of citizens ... an enormous amount of influence over the management and control of all public land in the state'.[67]

The JNF assumed 'three key roles': firstly, to serve as a 'large landholder'; secondly, to carry out 'specific tasks ... that were by their nature governmental functions'; and thirdly, to share 'responsibility with the state for managing Israel Lands'.[68] Prior to the recent reform (see below), the policy-setting Israel Lands Council had 22 members of which 10 were JNF appointees. The JNF itself directly manages 13 per cent of the state's land. Yet the JNF considers itself 'the caretaker of the land of Israel, on behalf of its owners – Jewish people everywhere'.[69]

When the Basic Law: Israel Lands was being presented, the Minister of Religious Affairs and Chairman of the Israeli Knesset Constitution, Law and Justice Committee said that 'the reasons for this proposed law, as I put it before you, are as follows: to give legal garb to a principle that is fundamentally religious, namely, "the land shall not be sold forever, for the land is mine" (Leviticus 25.23)'.[70] Fast forward six decades, and the situation remains that:

> The JNF, in relation to being an owner of land, is not a public body that works for the benefit of all citizens of the state. The loyalty of the JNF is given to the Jewish people and only to them is the JNF obligated. The JNF, as the owner of the JNF land, does not have a duty to practice equality towards all citizens of the state.[71]

The Jewish Agency (JA) also plays a role in Israel's administrative apartheid, principally in the way it is granted responsibilities for rural settlement and immigration. By the beginning of the 1980s, the JA had established over 800 agricultural settlements in 'close collaboration' with the government.[72] The fact that the JA and government work together on such substantial issues, shows that 'the Agency is in fact, if not in theory, a type of governmental authority'.[73] Yet the reality is that the JA's activities are 'confined to the Jewish sector'. Furthermore,

> there is no parallel governmental agency that deals with the same activities for those not covered by the WZO and Jewish Agency activities. The result is that an area such as new agricultural settlements in Israel is in effect restricted to the Jewish sector.[74]

Officials are well aware of the advantages that bodies like the JNF and JA bring. In 1987, the Attorney General said that if assistance for Jewish citizens returning from living abroad 'were to be given wholly by the Jewish Agency' it facilitates discrimination in a way that would not be possible 'if the assistance continues to be financed, in whole or in part, by the state'.[75] In 2002, commenting on a JA initiative to foster a 'Zionist majority' in the Negev, the then treasurer, Shai Hermesh, said that the reason for the plan is 'to get around the problem that the government must act on behalf of all citizens of the State of Israel while the WZO is entitled to act for the sake of the Jewish people'.[76]

In August 2009, the Knesset passed the Israel Land Administration Law. The emphasis of the land reform was privatisation, a result of Netanyahu's right-wing economic sensibilities and a sense that the present system was unwieldy and unresponsive to current Israeli housing needs. The bill that passed means the Israel Lands Administration is replaced by a new Land Authority, and allows for the privatisation of 200,000 acres of land (half by 2014).[77]

In May 2011 this transformation moved forward, with the total amount of affected land equalling 4 per cent of the ILA's holdings.[78] Crucially, the JNF has preserved its influential role, with representatives granted 6 of the 13 seats on the new Land Authority Council.[79] The chair of the budget committee will also be a JNF nominee.

In addition, the JNF will receive thousands of acres of land in the Negev and Galilee as a swap for its land in urban areas.[80] The agreement states that the Land Authority will administer the lands 'in a manner that will preserve the principles of the JNF relating to its lands'.[81] According to the JNF website, the reform allows the organisation to 'to continue to develop the land of Israel on behalf of its owners – Jewish people everywhere'.[82] The JNF also notes that the reform is the 'solution to the problem' of JNF's 'exposure' to 'lawsuits' – i.e. legal challenges to discrimination, a position it says is held by the Attorney General.

This is not the only problematic aspect of the land reform for Palestinians. With the privatisation, 'much of the land owned by the Palestinian refugees and internally-displaced persons' as well as other land 'confiscated from Palestinian citizens', can now 'be sold off under the law and placed beyond future restitution claims'.[83]

For some Israeli Knesset Members, however, placing land in the open market presented a risk. So in March 2011, an amendment was passed to the Israel Lands Law which prohibits 'the sale or transfer of state lands to foreigners'.[84] It is the definition of 'foreigners' which is interesting, since explicitly *excluded* from such a category are those 'entitled to immigrate to Israel under the Law of Return', i.e. Jews. In fact, limitations on the ability of foreigners to buy land in Israel already existed, but nevertheless, lawmakers made their intention clear when removing a clause that would have limited foreign Jews buying infrequently used second homes.

> We're here to prevent hostile takeover of the land, not to prevent a Jew who wants to purchase five apartments from doing so. Differentiating between Jews who plan to immigrate and those who don't is both impossible to do and goes against the foundations of Zionism.[85]

PLANNING SEGREGATION

In the 30 years following the establishment of the state of Israel, its Palestinian citizens lost a devastating amount of land. The consequences of the policy of expropriation and Judaisation (see Chapter 3) remain severe, and in fact have only got worse. Since 1948, the Palestinian minority has grown six-fold, while the land under its control has shrunk: comprising around 20 per cent of

Map 2 Jewish population centres (left to right) 1918, 1948, 1967, 2000. (arenaofspeculation.org, based on Malkit Shoshan, 'Atlas of the Conflict – Israel-Palestine')

the population, they privately own about 3.5 per cent of the state's total land.[86] In the last 60 years, the building density in Arab municipalities – remembering that 91 per cent of Palestinian citizens live in all-Arab communities – has increased 16-fold.[87]

Since 1948, over 700 Jewish communities have been established in Israel's pre-1967 borders. In the same period, not one new city, town or village for the Palestinian minority has been created, except for seven townships in the Negev intended to 'concentrate' the Bedouin population.[88] All this is compounded by systematic discrimination in the planning regime, on a local and national level.

Palestinian municipalities in Israel have jurisdiction over around 2.5 per cent of the area of the state. In the Galilee, despite making up over 70 per cent of the population, Palestinian municipalities have jurisdiction over just 16 per cent of the land.[89] These 'narrowly drawn' and 'restrictive jurisdictional boundaries' have served to create 'space for Jewish settlement and its expansion'.[90] Arrabe, for example, has village-owned

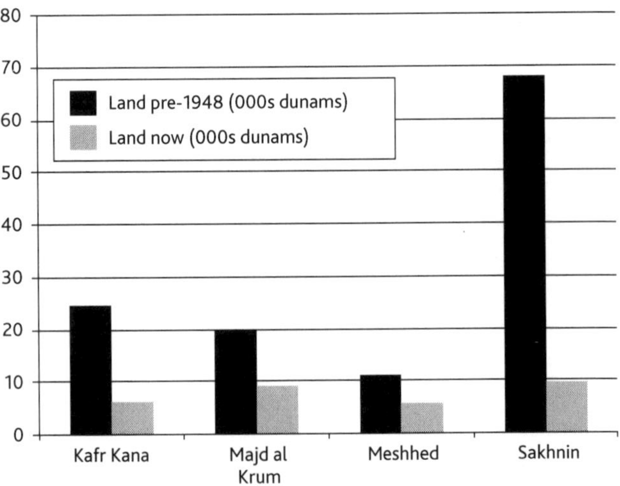

Figure 2 Municipal land loss for Arab communities in Israel. (Source: David A. Wesley, *State Practices & Zionist Images: Shaping Economic Development in Arab Towns in Israel*, Berghahn Books: Oxford, 2006)

land amounting to $30km^2$, yet its area of jurisdiction is only $9km^2$ and the master plan allows only $3km^2$ for development.[91] The Jewish development town of Upper Nazareth has jurisdiction over 19,200 dunams, for a population of 25,000; Palestinian Nazareth has 12,500 dunams for 65,000.[92]

Palestinian communities also suffer disproportionately from the lack of a 'master plan' – or are burdened by an inadequate, old one – without which it is impossible to get building permits. According to a 2010 study, around one in four Palestinian communities in Israel 'have neither a local nor privatized [planning] master plan'.[93] Since Palestinians are compelled to build 'illegally', they are also subject to home demolitions (see later in this chapter). A survey in the 1990s found that on average, it took seven years to prepare and approve an outline plan for a Jewish community in the Galilee; but 20 years for a Palestinian one.[94]

There is further discrimination and segregation-consolidating policies implemented at the level of regional councils. Out of the 53 regional councils in Israel, 50 of them contain Jewish localities, and the familiar pattern of unequal land allocation is repeated. In the Negev, the Abu Basma regional council responsible for Bedouin communities covers 34,000 dunams for a population of 30,000; while the B'nai Shimon regional council serves 5,900 citizens with jurisdiction over 450,000 dunams.[95] That amounts to 1.13 dunams per person in the Arab council and 76.3 dunams per person in the Jewish one.

Furthermore, the three Palestinian regional councils, 'unlike their Jewish counterparts', do not have 'territorial contiguity'.[96] Rather, 'they control only land within the village boundaries of the communities under the council's jurisdiction, while all the tracts of land between these villages belong to a neighbouring Jewish regional council'.[97] This fragmentation is an example of 'the thrust of Israel's planning policies' in the Galilee, namely, 'to maximize Jewish control over land and regional resources and weaken Arab attempts to challenge Jewish domination'.[98]

The Misgav Regional Council is a good example (see the section on Judaisation in Chapter 3). Created in the 1980s, it was 'given a highly irregular geographical shape, in order

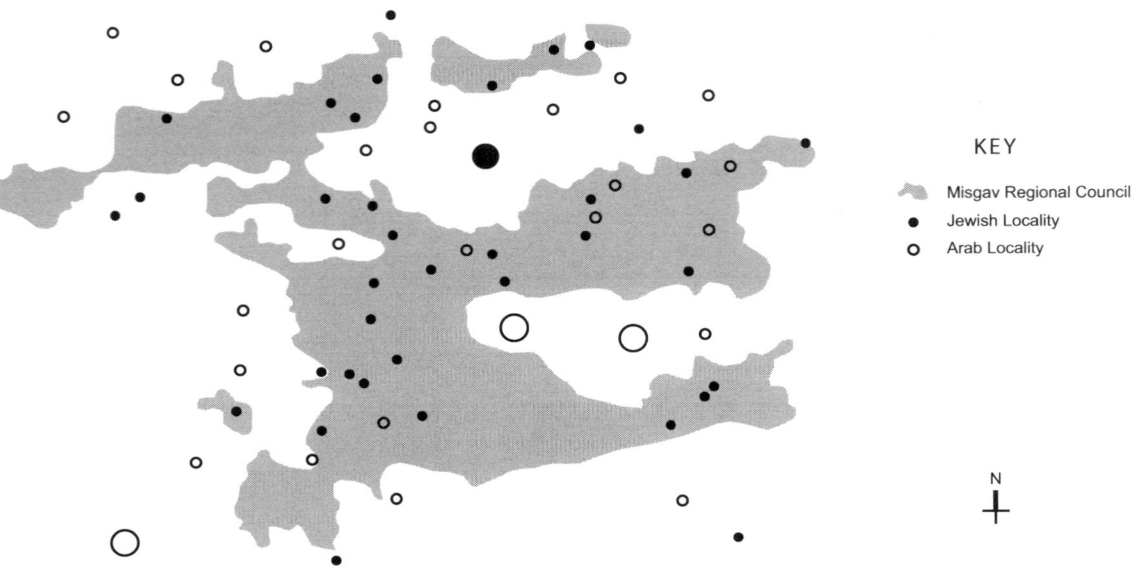

Map 3 Misgav Regional Council. (arenaofspeculation.org, based on Misgav Regional Council website, http://www.misgav.org.il/e/49/)

to include most Jewish settlements and exclude most Arab villages'. The result has been to reinforce 'patterns of functional and social segregation in the region, where nearly all services are provided on an ethnic basis'.[99] Misgav residents themselves, have recognised that theirs is 'not a regional plan in the ordinary sense', but 'a strategic plan ... to preserve state lands'.[100]

Finally, the character of the planning regime is replicated at a national level. In 2001, the Northern District Committee for Planning and Building submitted a revised plan for the Northern District, whose original goal in the 1980s was 'preserving the

'Ali Abu Sbeit

On 4 August 2003 Israeli security forces demolished the home of 'Ali and Sara Abu Sbeit and their six children, aged between 13 and two-and-a-half years, in Sa'wa, one of the unrecognised Bedouin villages.

'The police and border guards came at about 7 a.m. We were still asleep. There were more than 200 of them and they had bulldozers. They tied my hands behind my back and took me, my wife and the children out. They did not allow us time to take anything out of the house. Some policemen took out a few things but most of what we had remained in the house. They started to hit the house with the bulldozer and demolished it very quickly, then some of them clapped and they all left. It was a terrible day, my wife and the children were very sad, we were all very upset.

'This is the second time that my home has been demolished. The first time was in 1997 and I had to demolish the house myself; or else the authorities were going to make me pay the cost of the bulldozer and everything for the demolition ... We can't build anywhere, where are we supposed to live? After my house was demolished in 1997 my family and I lived with my mother for three years, but now there isn't space for all of us there. Then in 1999 I built this home, and now we are homeless again.'

Source: Amnesty International (2004) 'Under the rubble: house demolition and destruction of land and property'.

lands of the nation and Judaizing the Galilee'. The plan raised three 'problems' to be solved, including that: 'Jews constitute a minority in the north'; the 'Arab towns and villages are geographically contiguous'; and 'the taking control of land and illegal building,' referring unquestionably to the Arab population in the district.[101]

The plan for the Northern District deposited in 1999 did not even 'acknowledge the shortage of land for Arabs', even though the Palestinians make up half of the district and hold 6 per cent of the land. The plan did see fit, however, to note that the Jewish rural population had only 16 per cent of the land reserve while constituting 32 per cent of the population.[102]

UNRECOGNISED VILLAGES

The phenomenon of 'unrecognised villages' in Israel is a perfect microcosm of the way in which Palestinian citizens are, in more than one sense, 'wiped off the map'. Across the country, but mainly in the Negev, around 90,000 Palestinian citizens live in over 40 unrecognised villages, which the state refuses to legalise, and whose residents 'lack security of tenure and public services'.[103] Manipulating both planning legislation and the land claims process, 'the authorities simply pretended [these communities] were not there and categorised the land as agricultural or forestland, on which it is illegal to build homes'.[104]

While a few such villages have eventually won recognition, the vast majority continue to live under the threat of home demolitions and without access to basic services and infrastructure. Often, the government's response is to claim that since recognising villages means providing basic services, it is unfeasible to legalise small and isolated villages. In an interview in 2010, a negotiations manager at the government's 'Authority for the Regulation of Bedouin Settlements', said: 'If a village has a large enough population we will recognize it, but if the population is very small, say 400 or 500 people, we cannot do so'.[105]

Except that tiny Jewish communities are routinely authorised and connected. For example, in the 1990s, there were 53 official communities in Israel with less than 100 inhabitants – 51 of them Jewish, while 99 per cent of the more than 700 communities with fewer than 500 inhabitants are also Jewish.[106] Small Jewish settlements of a few dozen families – or even single family farms – are not a problem; but a Bedouin village with a population of several hundred is 'impractical'. Note that this is a pattern repeated in the West Bank, where tiny, Jewish colonies enjoy better infrastructure and services than Palestinians targeted for demolition or eviction.

In the last few years, the village of al-Araqib has come to represent the struggle of the unrecognised villages. The residents were expelled from their land in 1951, and like other Bedouin Palestinians, were confined to the 'Siyag' (fence) area. In the 1990s, al-Araqib families returned to their lands to fight for recognition. Now, however it is the target of an initiative by the state and Jewish National Fund intended to, in the words of Israel's then-agriculture minister, 'safeguard national lands'.[107]

At dawn on 27 July 2010, the Israeli authorities arrived to 'prepare the land for planting'.

> No less than 1,300 police officers began to demolish the homes while the residents tried to salvage their belongings. A helicopter flew above the village throughout the 13-hour demolition, which razed the 45 homes to the ground and uprooted around 4,500 olive trees.[108]

Since then, and at the time of writing, al-Araqib has been demolished more than 20 times; after each time, the residents rebuild. As a reporter for the *Jerusalem Post* noted in August 2010, 'the situation cannot go on indefinitely, especially as the powers-that-be in Israel have designated the land for a Jewish National Fund park'.[109] The day before the first demolition, Netanyahu warned in a government meeting that allowing 'for a region without a Jewish majority' in the Negev would pose 'a palpable threat' to Israel.[110]

North of the Negev, and a short drive from Tel Aviv, lies another unrecognised Palestinian community, Dahmash, situated between Lod and Ramle.[111] Dahmash has been inhabited since at least 1951, yet the authorities 'refuse to rezone the land as residential' – despite doing so for land nearby – and 'refuse to provide basic services such as paved roads, sewage, health facilities, kindergartens and schools'. Moreover, 'the authorities consider almost every one of the 70 houses 'illegal', and 13 are 'under threat of demolition'.[112]

Like in other cases, some of Dahmash's residents were given the land by the state 'as compensation for lands from which they had been displaced' in 1948 and 'to which the Israeli government prohibited them from returning'.[113] Since then, however, officials have refused to 'zone Dahmash for residential construction'. Many towns and neighbourhoods in central Israel, including the new residential development bordering Dahmash, were also originally zoned for agricultural use, but authorities rezoned those lands to allow them to expand and created plans that permitted residential construction. Neither regional nor national authorities have provided such a plan for Dahmash.

In the words of Human Rights Watch's deputy Middle East director: 'The 600 people of Dahmash are treated as if they don't exist, while Jewish towns are developed nearby in a way that threatens Dahmash residents' access to their homes and lands.'[114] As Arafat Ismayil, head of the Dahmash village committee, said to me, 'We're in the heart of Israel, but we're not here'.[115] Ramle's mayor, Yoel Lavi, 'who sits on the planning committee that rejected Dahmash's [alternative zoning] plan, told Israeli television in 2004 that the Maccabi District was not meant for Arabs because allowing Palestinian-Israeli citizens to live there would "harm the ability to market the project since people won't want to live there"'[116] In 2006, Lavi explained his own solution to the unrecognised village of Dahmash:

> take two D10 bulldozers, the kind the IDF uses in the Golan Heights, two border police units to secure the area, and go from one side to the other ... when you give the first shock with the crane everyone runs from their houses, don't worry.

Photograph 4 Demolished unrecognised village of Al-Araqib, Negev. (August 2010, Ariel Azoff)

Photograph 5 Al-Araqib 2. (October 2010, Ariel Azoff)

HOME DEMOLITIONS

The demolition of Palestinian homes is a widespread phenomenon in Israel, despite some people associating the practice solely with areas under military occupation, like East Jerusalem or the Jordan Valley. There may be legal and bureaucratic differences, but the same strategy is in place: restrict the ability of Palestinian communities to flourish and grow, while applying different, preferential standards to Jews.

Homes are demolished in both unrecognised villages and 'legal' Palestinian towns and villages (and indeed, in so-called 'mixed' towns). The unrecognised villages (see previous section) are understandably vulnerable given, in the eyes of the state, their illegality or at best ambiguous legality. Different statistics give a sense of the scale of the policy.

- Over 500 Bedouin homes demolished in the Negev, June 1988-May 1990.[117]
- Over 2000 Negev Bedouin homes demolished 1993–1996.[118]
- Over 600 Bedouin homes demolished 2001–2008.[119]

A key reason for such large number of home demolitions is the inadequate number of housing units being built for Palestinians. Between 1975 and 2000, for example, the number of public housing units built for the Palestinian minority was 0.3 per cent of the total.[120] A study on housing needs in 2005–09 conducted by the Arab Centre for Alternative Planning found that the Israel Land Administration (ILA) provided Palestinians with just 21 per cent of the needed land, while for Jewish citizens, 63 per cent of needs was met.[121] There is also a discrepancy in enforcement: in 1996, for example, 57 per cent of unlicensed building was carried out by Palestinians, but they constituted 90 per cent of all demolitions.[122]

Demolitions continue apace. In 2009, 165 buildings owned by Palestinian citizens were demolished, most of them in unrecognised villages in the Negev.[123] The Negev Coexistence Forum For Civil Equality recorded 30 separate demolition operations in the six months from October 2010 to March

2011, affecting over 20 houses and dozens of other structures.[124] In 2010, it was reported that the authorities had 'resolved to triple the demolition rate of illegal construction in the scattered Bedouin communities in the Negev'.[125]

Lod, a 'mixed city' in central Israel, is a good illustration of both the reality of demolitions and discrimination in planning, especially as it is not an 'unrecognised village' in the periphery of the country. In this city ten miles from Tel Aviv, as many as 3,000 homes are considered 'illegal', and thus under constant threat of demolition. These 'illegal' homes constitute around 15 per cent of the total houses in the city, and as much as half of all Palestinian homes.[126] Responding to the municipality's reason for demolitions – that the homes lack permits – Human Rights Watch noted how 'such permits' are 'repeatedly refused'.[127] Moreover, land *is* 'rezoned' from agricultural to residential when it comes to building 'a housing development ... for Israeli security service personnel' and 'a Jewish religious college'. 'Israeli authorities

Hani Khawaja

Hani Khawaja, 54, a lifelong resident of the Arab neighbourhood in Lod, tells his story with the help of fellow Lod resident Khalil Aby Shehadi.

'To demolish a house, it costs a lot of money. It's about half a million shekels, that's about $150,000. When they come, they bring the police with them. They close the two entrances to the neighborhood,' said Shehadi. 'We can't go to school, we can't go to the hospital, we can't go anywhere. At 4:30 in the morning, they closed the neighborhood. They put police everywhere, on horses, on cars, on foot. And helicopters. There were 250 policemen.'

'They – he and his small children, tried to take everything out of their house. They took them out by force,' continued Shehadi. 'They destroyed the house with everything in it. Schoolbags, books, everything! Refrigerator, everything! Everything, yes.'

Source: Mary Slosson, 'Arab in Israel: two stories from Lod', *Neon Tommy*, 28 April 2011

allow buildings that will benefit Jewish citizens while demolishing Arab houses next door. That obviously discriminates against non-Jewish Israelis, but officials haven't given any justification for this clear difference in treatment between citizens.'

ADMISSIONS COMMITTEES

Until recently, so-called admissions committees in small Israeli communities have got little attention, despite the fact that they have served as a key tool in the exclusion of Palestinian citizens, the maintenance of segregation, and Jewish control over rural land. Admissions committees set the criteria and act as a 'filter' for who can live in around 70 per cent of all the communities in Israel, including 85 per cent of those in rural areas.[128] In addition, these communities come under the jurisdiction of 52 regional councils which together cover 80 per cent of the state's territory. In other words, they are a means by which a small number of people – about 5 per cent of the population – can exercise control over a significant amount of land.

The passing of legislation by the Netanyahu-Lieberman coalition formalising their role has raised their profile, but this 'filter' system has been in operation in Israel for decades. According to a 2008 Human Rights Watch report, admissions – or 'selection' – committees 'determine who can gain admittance to all communities of fewer than 500 households'.[129]

> The selection is based on vague criteria including 'appropriate to social life in a small community' for which applicants must provide 'an opinion of a professional institute which will examine whether they fit the social life of the community'. Selection committees are made up of government and community representatives as well as a senior official in the Jewish Agency or the Zionist Organization, and have notoriously been used to exclude Arabs from living in rural Jewish communities.

Former head of education for the Jewish Agency, David Harman, described the process candidly to Bernard Avishai in the latter's book *The Hebrew Republic*: 'Could Arabs expect to become part of the housing project? I asked. "Don't bother applying," Harman said.'[130]

In 1997, Palestinian citizen Aadel Suad heard almost exactly the same thing from the senior official of the planning committee for Misgav Local Council: 'Don't waste your time. We'll keep you waiting for 30 years.'[131]

Before coming to the most recent legislative developments, it is worth highlighting an earlier attempt to legislate the exclusionary role of admissions committees. In July 2002, with Ariel Sharon as Prime Minister, the Israeli cabinet voted 17–2 in favour of a bill that barred Palestinian citizens 'from buying homes in Jewish communities built on state land'.[132] The context of the initiative was to undermine a potentially-threatening Supreme Court ruling in 2000, when Palestinian citizen Adel Kaadan was judged to have suffered unlawful discrimination in being rejected by an admissions committee, as well as to support a government policy 'that recognizes the need to Judaize various areas across the country'. Yet just days later, despite an overwhelming cabinet majority, the government backed down, deciding to 'bury the bill' in the face of the controversy.[133]

But there were no such qualms when the Netanyahu-Lieberman coalition began the process of introducing new legislation on admissions committees. In December 2009, the Knesset overwhelmingly approved in a preliminary vote the decision of the Ministerial Committee on Legislative Affairs 'to allow admission committees in the Galilee and Negev to filter candidates seeking to live in their communities'.[134] The bill's sponsors were clear about the rationale for the proposal, with (Member of Knesset) MK David Rotem commenting, 'Don't blame us for wanting to preserve Israel as a Jewish state', and MK Yisrael Hasson saying the proposal was aimed at 'preserving the ability to fulfil the Zionist dream'.[135] Deputy Foreign Minister Danny Ayalon also defended the law: 'The conquest of land is still important today to the nation as well as Zionism, and we shouldn't be ashamed of it.'[136]

As the bill progressed through the Knesset, this kind of rhetoric was never far behind. In January 2010, MK Rotem 'joked' that in his opinion, 'every Jewish town needs at least one Arab' since 'what would happen if my refrigerator stopped working on a Saturday?'[137] In February 2011, bill co-sponsor MK Shai Hermesh – a member of the supposedly 'centrist' Kadima party – said, 'it's not discrimination ... but we should not be mixed together'.[138] MK Rotem said that he believed Jews and Arabs could be 'separate but equal'.

When the law finally passed, the number of applicable communities was reduced, and a clause had been inserted prohibiting discrimination. Yet the intentionally vague wording of the law means that a potential resident can be refused for a 'lack of compatibility with the social-cultural fabric' of the community. Moreover, the law confirms the presence on each committee of a representative of the Jewish Agency or World Zionist Organisation – two groups committed to privileging Jews (see Chapter 1). This example of 'officially sanctioned discrimination', in the words of Human Rights Watch, 'formalizes the compilation of such committees' in four out of ten towns in Israel, and thus has instituted 'an apartheid-like regime in housing'.[139]

3
Judaisation and the Demographic Threat

The project of 'Judaizing the Galilee' commenced when the state was founded and has continued in various guises to the present day ...[1]

Professor Hillel Cohen, Hebrew University of Jerusalem

The Judaization project is driven by the Zionist premise that Israel is a territory and a state that 'belongs' to, and only to, the Jewish people.[2]

Dr Haim Yacobi, Ben-Gurion University

After the ethnic cleansing in 1947–49, the Palestinians who had managed to remain in the new Jewish state were mainly concentrated in the Galilee and Negev. Since 1948, these two regions have remained areas of 'strategic concern' for the Israeli state on account of their proportionally higher number of Palestinians, and the focus of a strategic goal aimed at 'spatial Judaisation'. This approach to state and regional planning policy is based on the premise that there can be 'too many' of the 'wrong' kind of citizen in a particular area. As such, it is closely related to the discourse of 'demographic threat', a routine way to describe the Palestinian minority, and the everyday expression of racism towards Palestinian citizens by politicians and the general public. This chapter will examine the Judaisation of the Galilee and Negev, but first, will contextualise these policies within Israel's all-prevalent demography discourse.

THE DEMOGRAPHIC THREAT

Talk of a 'demographic threat' is not legitimate. Imagine what would happen if a discussion were held in the United States or Europe on 'the worrisome natural growth of the Jews'.[3]

The practical policies of Judaisation are informed by the mainstream Israeli discourse that sees Palestinian citizens as a 'demographic threat'. Describing one group of citizens as a 'threat' based on their ethno-religious identity sounds shocking, but in so far as it relates to the Zionist project of creating and maintaining Jewish hegemony in Palestine/Israel, there is a logical consistency. A good example of the weight this idea carries in the Israeli political-military establishment is the Herzliya Conference in 2000, the first in what has become an annual gathering of the political and security elite in Israel, as well as academics and politicians from around the world. In 2001, the conference was sponsored by institutions like the Jewish Agency, Defense Ministry and National Security Council, and participants 'were said to constitute a veritable who's who of the Israeli establishment (government, security, academic, business, and media) as well as Jewish leaders from the United States and elsewhere'.[4]

The subsequent conference report said that 'the demographic trends in Israel and its surroundings and their ramifications pose a severe threat to Israel in terms of its character and identity as a Jewish state belonging to the Jewish people'. As a consequence, recommendations included Judaisation of the Galilee and Negev, as well as 'granting Israeli Arabs a choice between full citizenship in the State of Israel and citizenship in the Palestinian state'.

Eighteen months after the publication of the Herzliya Conference report, the Israel Council for Demography convened 'after five years of inactivity'. The brief was to draw up guidelines for policies designed to 'preserve Israel's Jewish character'.[5] At the opening meeting, Labour and Social Affairs Minister Shlomo Benizri spoke of 'the beauty of the Jewish family that is blessed with many children', and how

> We are the majority in this country and we have the right to preserve our image and the image of the Jewish state, and also to preserve the Jewish people. Every state has the full right to preserve its character.[6]

In another example in April 2005, it was reported that the National Security Council had 'formulated a plan for "improving the demographic situation in Israel"'. The article contextualised 'the plan' as coming 'amid estimates regarding the growth rate of the Arab-Israeli minority'.[7]

In Israel, then, to consider ethnic minority citizens to be an intrinsic 'threat' to the country is mainstream, state-supported politics. Benjamin Netanyahu, as Finance Minister in 2003, said Palestinian citizens constitute the real 'demographic problem'.[8] In 2010, the chair of the Knesset's Ethics committee warned that 'the Jews must stop burying their heads in the sand and recognize that the Arabs in Israel are our enemy'.[9] The same year, Mayor of Jerusalem Nir Barkat described the Palestinians in the city as a 'strategic threat'; his predecessor Ehud Olmert told reporters in 1998 that 'it's a matter of concern when the non-Jewish population rises a lot faster than the Jewish population'.[10]

This is not just a question of rhetoric. In 2002, Israel's Interior Minister 'instructed ministry legal advisers to look into ways of changing legislation in order to reduce the number of Arabs who receive Israeli citizenship by marrying Israeli citizens'. Again the 'context' was the rising number of non-Jewish citizens, as a result of which 'the Jewish character of the state is being endangered' (see also the section on the separation of spouses in Chapter 1).[11]

In 2004, *Ha'aretz* reported a drop in the 'Israeli Arab birthrate', a development attributed to 'cutbacks in child support allocations'. At the same time as claiming that these cutbacks were not for 'demographic reasons', the report also cites 'a senior Finance Ministry official' who said that as a result of the 'internal demographic threat': 'We are reversing the graph, to defend the Jewish majority in the country.'[12]

A week later, the same newspaper reported how 'senior government officials' had tried to persuade leaders of the Religious Zionist Shas party to enter the coalition by assuring them that cuts to child allowances was not meant to hurt the ultra-Orthodox, 'only' the Arabs.[13]

Some of the 'demographic threat' discourse explicitly describes the 'threat' posed by the Palestinian minority in military or existential terms. At the 2006 Herzliya conference, an IDF reserve Brigadier General warned:

> If we don't do something the partition plan of 1947 will materialize right in front of our eyes. It has in fact already begun. There is a connection from Lebanon through the Galilee to Jenin and the triangle [an area with a large number of Palestinian residents].[14]

Senior politicians are perfectly comfortable raising the specter of a 'fifth column'. Danny Ayalon, who went on to become Deputy Foreign Minister, told a press conference in September 2008 that the lack of a 'Jewish majority in the north' meant the risk that 'the Arab majority' would 'declare independence', and ultimately 'lead to the dismantling of the State of Israel'.[15] In a government meeting in August 2010, Prime Minister Netanyahu compared the 'palpable threat' of a 'region without a Jewish majority' to what 'happened in the Balkans'.[16]

ROUTINE RACISM

There is also a cruder, anti-Arab racism in Israeli society, as evidenced in polls, and by the ability of public officials, both nationally and locally, to express hateful bigotry without risk of serious censure. Here are just a few examples:

> There are Arab citizens in the State of Israel. This is our greatest sorrow.
>
> Public Security Minister Gideon Ezra, 2004.[17]

> What is it about Islam as a whole and the Palestinians in particular? Is it some form of cultural deprivation? Is it some genetic defect? There is something that defies explanation in this continued murderousness.
>
> Deputy Defense Minister Ze'ev Boim, 2004.[18]

> I see [it] as a national duty to prevent the spread of a population [the Arabs] that, to say the least, does not love the state of Israel ... If we go on like we have until now, we will lose the Galilee. Populations that should not mix are spreading there.
>
> Housing Minister Ariel Atias, 2009.[19]

> Bedouin are a bloodthirsty people who commit polygamy, have 30 children, and continue to expand their illegal settlements by taking over state lands. In their culture, they relieve themselves outdoors and don't even know how to use the toilet.
>
> Head of the Educational Authority for Bedouins, Moshe Shohat, 2001.[20]

> We must launch incentives, even offering money to encourage their [Bedouin citizens] return to the countries they came from. Today there is a lot of land in Saudi Arabia and in Libya, too – there's lots of land in lots of places.
>
> Chief Rabbi of Hebron, at municipality-sponsored Ramle Conference, 2011.[21]

> The delivery rooms in Soroka Hospital in Be'er Sheva have turned into a factory for the production of a backward population.
>
> Dr Yitzhak Ravid, Armament Development Authority, Herzliya Conference, 2003.[22]

> The leaders of the city should stop this invasion before the city is no longer Zionist and nationalist ... I am not a racist and I have never been one, but many Jewish families are afraid that Arabs will start relationships with their daughters.
>
> Councillor Avraham Maman, Nazaret Illit, 2004.[23]

> We want to Judaize the Wadi Ara area ... The state wants to put this place in order so that the Arabs won't rear their heads.
>
> Nissim Dahan, Interior Ministry-appointed head of local council, 2008.[24]

There is even official toleration or encouragement of groups that seek to prevent Jewish-Arab dating or marriages.[25] In 2011, a rally in Ashkelon against 'Arabs who associate with [Jewish] girls' was led by a city councillor.[26] The year before, the municipality of Petah Tikva set up a 'task force' to 'patrol the city at night and break up Arab-Jewish dates'.[27]

This kind of discourse can find a home in the Knesset: in February 2011, the Committee for the Advancement of Women held a hearing on the need to 'combat intermarriage' – specifically between 'Jewish women and Arab men'.[28] One Jewish woman who 'testified' before the committee said that 'marriages between Jewish women and Muslim men are like water and oil ... there are differences in mentalities that are impossible to deny'.

Opinion polls of the Jewish Israeli public regularly display deep-seated levels of anti-Arab racism. Again, these are just a few examples:

> Over half of Jewish Israelis say marriage to an Arab is 'equal to national treason'.[29]
>
> 78 per cent of Jewish Israelis oppose Arabs joining the government.[30]
>
> 62 per cent of Jewish Israelis support encouraging the emigration of Palestinian citizens.[31]
>
> 36 per cent of Jewish Israelis are in favor of revoking the voting rights of non-Jews.[32]

JUDAISING THE GALILEE

> As a rule, all of Upper Nazareth is built on expropriated land – whether this way or that – and the original owners are still here. Just the other day, one came here and cried about his eighteen dunams that the new hotel is built on. The idea was Judaization of Galilee – and that means taking land. There was no land that wasn't cultivated or that wasn't claimed.[33]

A good example of the way in which the preoccupation with demography, racism, and the Judaisation policies connect is the Koenig Report, a leaked internal document written in 1976 by Israel Koenig, a senior official in the Minister of Interior. With its focus on the 'demographic problem' in the Galilee, here is how *Time* magazine covered the document at the time:

> Infiltration by secret agents. Reprisals against 'negative' citizens. Systematic job discrimination and measures to encourage emigration.

> To many Israelis, it all sounded like a prescription for a pogrom against Jews. In fact, they were an Israeli civil servant's proposals for controlling Israel's exploding Arab population.[34]

Koenig suggested that the Israeli government 'expand and deepen Jewish settlement in areas where the contiguity of the Arab population is prominent' and 'limit "breaking of new ground" by Arab settlements'.[35] Although the furore pushed Israeli government figures to distance themselves from the report, the denials were a transparent PR exercise, particularly, as the Palestinian mayor of Nazareth at the time Tawfiq Zayyad pointed out, 'Many of Koenig's recommendations are already official policy'.[36] Moreover, the Interior Ministry's Director-General defended 'a Jewish majority' in the Galilee as 'a legitimate goal', the proposals were endorsed by 'prominent Jewish politicians from the Galilee', and the memorandum's co-author was picked by Yitzhak Rabin 'as his candidate for appointment as director of the Labor Party's Arab Department'.[37]

There is then a direct link between the 'demography discourse' and specific policies intended to contribute towards the Judaisation of the Galilee. Because of the 'rhetorical inconvenience' of a 'slogan' like 'Judaise the Galilee', Labor government spokespersons have 'tended to substitute other phrases' like 'populate the Galilee' or 'develop the Galilee''.[38] Yet, 'the crucial concern remains making and keeping the Galilee Jewish.' As Israeli journalist Noam Sheizaf put it recently, 'viewing Jewish hegemony as a necessity is something that all Zionist parties have in common', and that while there are differences between Labor and Lieberman, 'all of them share the demographic obsession'.[39]

The first element of the Judaisation drive has been the confiscation of Palestinian property and land in the target regions. The methods and legislation used to advance this end were discussed in Chapter 2. One law worth singling out in this context is the Land (Acquisition for Public Purposes) Ordinance of 1943, whose use by the Israeli state to carry out Judaisation is instructive. The Public Purposes Ordinance has been the instrument by which some of the most substantial land expropriations have been carried out, including the land used to create Upper Nazareth. This brings in the second element in the Judaisation project – the establishment of Jewish communities in areas where Palestinian citizens are more numerous.

Upper Nazareth exemplifies this process. Having confiscated land 'in the public interest' in the mid 1950s, the Israeli government created Upper Nazareth, overlooking Nazareth, the largest Palestinian city inside Israel's pre-1967 borders. In 1953, a government official acknowledged that 'making Nazareth a partially Jewish city' would be 'a colonizing act with difficulties', but its importance was also clear.[40] The director of the IDF Planning Department said that the role of Upper Nazareth would be to 'emphasize and safeguard the Jewish character of the Galilee as a whole', while according to the Northern Military Governor, the final aim of the settlement was to 'swallow up' the Arab city through 'growth of the Jewish population around a hard-core group'.[41]

In a 1957 letter reproduced in a publication marking the Jewish town's thirtieth anniversary, the then Prime Minister, Ben Gurion, wrote that 'the new settlement must be a Jewish town that will assert a Jewish presence in the area'.[42] In the mid 1960s, an Israeli newspaper article described the creation of Upper Nazareth as a governmental decision 'to impose on Arab Nazareth a Jewish town ... whose purpose – whose basic, primary, and even sole purpose is 'to break' Arab autonomy in the region and in this city, and later, to create a Jewish majority'.[43]

Today, while Upper Nazareth's 50,000 inhabitants occupy 42,000 dunams, down the hill in Nazareth, 70,000 Palestinians are forced into just 14,000 dunams: four times as crowded.[44] Yet ironically, it is precisely this lack of room for expansion that has forced those Palestinians who can afford it to move to Upper Nazareth. This is the context for more recent efforts intended to consolidate the city's 'Jewishness', like the announcement in June 2009 of a new ultra-Orthodox neighbourhood 'to counter Arabs moving in'.[45] A month later, Rabbi Dov Lior, chair of the Yesha Rabbis Council, called for 'the public to act to "Judaize"' Upper Nazareth.[46]

This is the context for the rhetoric used by Upper Nazareth mayor (at the time of writing) Shimon Gapso. Here are a selection of his public remarks on Upper Nazareth's 'Jewishness' and the question of Judaisation:

> I am all for a democratic Upper Nazareth, but first of all a Jewish one.[47]

> It is time to call a spade a spade. Just as Ben-Gurion and Peres said in the 1950s that the Galilee must be Jewish, we say the same about Nazareth Illit: It must retain its Jewish character .... The primary goal is to put the brakes on the demographic deterioration ...[48]

> Upper Nazareth is a Jewish town and all its symbols are Jewish. As long as I hold office, no non-Jewish symbol will be presented in the city.[49]

> There is a difference between observing your religion and creating a provocation, and I'm going back to the matter of the noise of the mosques.[50]

Another example of the drive to move more Jews to the Galilee was the establishment of mitzpim (lookout) settlements beginning in the late 1970s. The Jewish Agency was 'the driving force' behind this initiative, which by the end of the 1980s had established several dozen such communities.[51] The Jewish Agency for Israel describes the background frankly on its website:

> In large areas of the north, where Jewish settlement was fairly scarce, there was a substantial Arab minority. Occasional discomfort had been expressed over the situation through the years; Menachem Begin's first government decided that the time had come to act. A plan was developed for a series of settlements, called Mitzpim (look-outs), to be placed on the higher topographical points of the areas defined as priorities.[52]

JA documents that preceded the initiative carried the same message, speaking 'of the need to deploy Jewish rural settlement in the large areas still without a Jewish presence', while another claimed that the new settlement programme would 'save State land from Arab invaders'.[53] As a member of the JA's 'hilltop planning team' put it more recently, the goals were clear: 'to prevent Arabs from 'taking over' government lands, keep Arab villages from attaining territorial continuity and attract a 'strong' population to the Galilee'.[54]

The entire discourse of the *mitzpim*, from their very name to the emphasis on 'conquest' and 'redemption' of land, was shaped by militarism and ethno-purity, with Israel's own citizens – the Palestinians – the target of the 'operation'. Descriptions of this state-JA partnership emphasise the same aim: 'to block the growth of adjacent Arab communities' and 'break the continuity of the Arab population in the region'.[55] In 2004, *Ha'aretz* reported on a University of Haifa study that set out to assess the success of the *mitzpim*.

> Without mincing words, the study reveals that underlying the project were principles of ethnic discrimination, demographic phobia, and the concept that the country's Arab citizens are not equals but constitute a threat to its existence.[56]

JUDAISING THE NEGEV

> The policy of Israel in the Negev and in other areas of the country is to 'Judaise' the land. It does not mean that others will not exist here at all. It means Jewish settlements are favoured.
>
> Professor Yanni Nevo, Ben-Gurion University.[57]

The Negev, or al-Naqab in Arabic, is an area that has been consistently targeted by Israeli governments, along with agencies like the Jewish National Fund (JNF), for so-called 'development', i.e. Judaisation. In parallel to the indigenous Bedouin Palestinians being expelled and forcibly relocated (see Chapter 2), private resources have been mobilised in order to 'settle' the Negev with Jews. As a Human Rights Watch report put it in 2008, 'the state's motives' for 'discriminatory, exclusionary and punitive policies' in the Negev 'can be elicited from policy documents and official rhetoric'.[58] The Israeli state's aim: 'maximising its control over Negev land and increasing the Jewish population in the area for strategic, economic and demographic reasons'. Professor Oren Yiftachel of Ben-Gurion University has put it bluntly: 'the government wants to de-Arabise the land'.[59]

In 2003, the then Prime Minister, Ariel Sharon, announced a new initiative calling for 30 new towns, most in the Galilee and Negev.[60] Apparently, Sharon had concluded that after investing in 'settling the [occupied] territories' it was now 'necessary to settle the Galilee and the Negev'. At the time, the PM's Adviser on 'Settlement Affairs' told a radio station that a key issue 'in the establishment of these settlements' is to locate them 'in places that are important to the state, that is, for Jewish settlement; in other words, 'to strengthen settlement in areas sparse in Jewish population'.[61]

Just the previous year, in the context of a different plan to establish 14 new communities, Sharon told a government meeting: 'If we do not settle the land, someone else will do so'.[62] In the lead up to Israel's evacuation of its colonies from the Gaza Strip in 2005, President George W. Bush wrote in a letter to Sharon how in the context of the 'disengagement plan', the US understood the importance of bringing 'new opportunities to the Negev and the Galilee'.[63] Discussing the aid Israel sought from the US to 'cover the costs' of disengagement, American-Jewish newspaper *Forward* noted that an Israeli government goal – 'less explicit when pitched in Washington' – is to 'solidify a Jewish majority' in the Negev and Galilee.[64]

The Negev is the location for classic, unfiltered Zionist frontier discourse. The Jewish National Fund in the UK talks about supporting 'the pioneers who are bringing the desert to life', while the JNF in Israel boast of their 'major role' in 'redeeming and reclaiming land'.[65] An article in the Zionist magazine *B'Nai B'Rith* called the Negev 'the closest thing to the tabula rasa [literally "blank slate"] many of Israel's pre-state pioneers found when they first came to the Holy Land'.[66] In the space where 'redemption' meets 'tabula rasa', is the rhetoric of Bedouin Palestinian citizens as a threat.

In 2002, then-National Infrastructure Minister Avigdor Lieberman said:

> We must stop their illegal invasion into state land by all means possible ... one of my main missions is to return power to the Land Authority in dealing with the non-Jewish threat to our lands. At the same time, we must settle the land by building new communal settlements and family farms. If we don't do this, we shall lose the Negev forever.[67]

This is a theme returned to repeatedly, even if sometimes in less blunt terms. Avishai Braverman (at the time the President of Ben-Gurion University – who went on to became Minister for Minority Affairs) said in 2004 that 'if Zionism is a motivating force, then it needs to travel south to the Negev, so that Israel does not turn into a Palestinian State'. Shmuel Rifman, chair of the Ramat HaNegev regional council, a crucial partner-authority in 'developing' the Negev, expressed his frustration at what he sees as state inaction: 'Wherever Jews try to put down stakes, the Bedouin suddenly appear.'[69] Ariel Sharon, just before becoming Prime Minister, published an article in which he wrote:

> In the Negev, we face a serious problem: About 900,000 dunams of government land are not in our hands, but in the hands of the Bedouin population ... It is, essentially, a demographic phenomenon ... The Bedouin are grabbing new territory. They are gnawing away at the country's land reserves, and no one is doing anything significant about it.[70]

Thus the establishment of new Jewish communities in the Negev is often explicitly tied to countering the Bedouin presence. In 2004, *Ha'aretz* reported how the government's Housing Ministry team had described a planned settlement as 'prevent[ing] the expansion of the Bedouin community northward'.[71] At an Interior Ministry meeting, 'participants talked of blocking the Bedouin expansion', but also 'agreed this terminology could not be used in official documents'. One official present said that 'some things should not be declared out loud'.

The Israeli government pursues the Judaisation of the Negev by partnering with other interested parties, like the Jewish Agency (JA). This relationship goes back a long way: in the mid 1970s an official from the JA's Land Settlement Department spoke of a 'plan' to establish 'villages ... [that] would be for Jews only'.[72]

Three decades later, and the JA announce plans to 'encourage' 350,000 people to move to the Galilee and Negev combined, in order to guarantee a 'Zionist majority' in those areas.[73] A few months later, the JA's Treasurer Shai Hermesh linked the initiative for a 'Zionist majority' with 'the demographic problem' in Israel's north and south.[74]

Another key organisation involved is the JNF, whose chair told the Israeli press in 2001 that 'unsettled land is occupied by Bedouin' in the Negev and Galilee.[75] In 2010, the chief executive of JNF in the US, Russell Robinson, expressed his concern that 'if we don't get 500,000 people to move to the Negev in the next five years, we're going to lose it'.[76] To what – or whom – went unsaid. Some years earlier, Robinson was clearer about the consequences of the JNF's 'project to remake' the demographics: 'such an influx' of Jews would mean 'a certain amount of displacement' for the Bedouin.[77]

But it's not just the 'national institutions' like the JA and JNF. In 2009, the Deputy Foreign Minister, Danny Ayalon, organised a conference at the Knesset to announce a 'new umbrella council' for NGOs that 'promote settling the periphery'.[78] Lest there be any doubt what aim these groups had in common, Ayalon spelled it out:

> There are those inside and outside Israel who are trying to disconnect the Negev and Galilee from the country. If there is no Jewish majority in these areas, they will be in danger, because there are those who could ask for autonomy.

Another strategy used in the Negev is so-called 'individual settlements', more than 50 of which have been established, occupying over 80,000 dunams of land. Many of these were created 'without permits and in violation of the planning and building laws and regulations'.[79] Given to Jewish families, 'the real, but unacknowledged, reason' – in the words of *Ha'aretz* – for the state's support of such settlements 'is the view that it constitutes a barrier to Bedouin and Arab expansion in the Negev and in Galilee'.[80] In fact, this role is not always 'unacknowledged': in 1997, as director of the Prime Minister's

Office, Avigdor Lieberman described the 'purpose' of the 'plan to encourage individual settlement in the problem areas' as 'being to safeguard the land'.[81] In a draft report prepared for the Prime Minister's office, a reason given for individual settlements is 'to preserve state lands' as a solution 'for demographic issues'.[82]

To advance the goal of 'block[ing] the Bedouin expansion', in the last ten years, the Israeli government has promoted what is referred to as the 'Wine Route', a project intended to connect 30-plus individually-owned farms as part of a tourism initiative. This has involved 'retroactively legalizing existing settlements', and making provision for new ones.[83] In November 2010, the Knesset passed an amendment to the 1991 Negev Development Authority Law, which recognised individual settlements and authorised the allocation of more land for further such development.[84] Israeli Professor Neve Gordon highlighted the Israeli government's clear double standard:

> For years, Israeli officials have emphasized the need to concentrate the 75,000 Bedouins in large townships, stating that their forty-five villages are too small and scattered along a fairly large area, making it very difficult to provide them with infrastructure. This served to justify the policy of not recognizing them. And yet now, the very same officials are handing out permits to scores of scattered farms, which stretch across thousands of dunams (a dunam is approximately a quarter of an acre), each one home to a single family.[85]

INCENTIVES

Another aspect of the Judaisation project is the use of government incentives to encourage Jewish Israelis to move to the Negev and Galilee. In 2003, the Prime Minister signed off on a decision to give demobilised soldiers a huge discount for property leasing fees.[86] The intention of this 'generous initiative', in the words of *Ha'aretz* correspondent Akiva Eldar, was 'to promote settlement in small communities (up to 500 housing units) located in the Negev and Galilee within areas designated national priority areas'. Eldar noted that 'the requirement of 12 months' service as a condition for receiving the benefit is enough to ensure that national lands in sensitive areas do not wind up in Arab hands'.

In 2010, the government revealed plans for IDF combat troops to be 'allocated land upon discharge'.[87]

> Land will be allocated in the Galilee, the Negev desert, the Jordan Valley and the Golan Heights – with the result that the move is likely to be seen as a continuation of the government's controversial policy of encouraging Israeli Jews to reside in rural regions with large Arab populations.

Later that year, Israel's cabinet approved draft legislation to 'grant benefits to discharged soldiers in order to encourage them to study at institutions of higher learning in the periphery'.[88] Discussing these various initiatives, Deputy Minister for the Development of the Negev and the Galilee Ayoub Kara commented that: 'This is our opportunity to change the demographics. If we don't pursue this we will find ourselves with more Arabs than Jews in these areas.'[89]

IN SUMMARY

Israel's Judaisation policies in the Negev and Galilee follow the same priorities as the colonial occupation of East Jerusalem and the West Bank. This linkage is made by Israeli officials themselves, as well as by organisations like the Jewish Agency, whose Settlement Department 'intentionally does not distinguish' between the Occupied Territories and Israel 'proper'.[90] In a 2006 interview the 'adviser to the prime minister on settlements' Uzi Keren was 'at pains to stress his commitment to bolstering the Jewish population of the Golan, the Galilee and the Negev, along with his concern for the West Bank and Gaza settlers', since, in his own words, 'settlement is settlement'.[91] Keren noted approvingly the policy pursued by Sharon of creating 'new settlements in the Galilee' in order to 'demographically strengthen' the area.

This has also been a policy pursued by Israeli politicians across the party divide. Ehud Barak identifies the Labor Party's 'priorities' as 'the Galilee, the Negev and the periphery', while Kadima's Jacob Edery can state that 'we have to do everything we can to boost Jewish population in the Galilee'.[92] Likud's Silvan Shalom, in his capacity as Minister for Development of the Negev and Galilee, wants 'to encourage 300,000 Israelis to move to the Negev and an equal number to the Galilee by 2020', and Yisrael Beiteinu's Danny Ayalon believes that 'the focus for today is to Judaize the Negev and the Galilee'.[93]

Between the early 1960s and the 1990s, the proportion of Jewish citizens in the population of Galilee increased by more than three-fold.[94] Yet for many, like Upper Nazareth mayor, the 'demographic threat' remains very much alive: 'The State of Israel's plan was that 45% of the Galilee will be Jewish by 2010. In reality, we are less than 40%, and if the State doesn't make sure to bring Jews here en masse, we will lose the Galilee.'[95] The unpleasant reality for the country's Palestinian minority is that 'the Judaization of space is at the heart of Israel's ethno-national regime'.[96]

4
Systematic Discrimination

The Israeli state's identification as 'Jewish' has an impact on its Palestinian minority beyond the core issues of land, housing, and citizenship. The discrimination affects a number of other aspects of ordinary life, from municipal budgets to the education sector. The following chapter is an introduction to some of these issues which, although some try, cannot be successfully tackled independently of the broader system of segregation and exclusion maintained by the Israeli state.

NATIONAL PRIORTITY AREAS

'National Priority Areas' (NPA) is a designation granted by the Israeli government to certain regions (including settlements in the occupied Palestinian territories) in order to allocate generous economic benefits and incentives to particular communities. In line with the long-standing strategic aim of Judaising the north and south (see Chapter 3), large swathes of the Galilee and Negev have typically been marked as NPA, yet this has been done in a way that channels funding to Jewish areas and excludes Palestinians.

For example, in 1995 in northern Israel, 'certain municipalities or industrial areas' were given 'exceptional status, raised by one degree above that of the geographic area in which they are situated' – all of them 'Jewish localities'.[1] A government report made public in 2003 'detailed description of the income tax benefits granted' to those in NPA regions in the north, Negev, and West Bank (i.e. settlers), with *Ha'aretz* reporting how 'the document also notes that these benefits are granted for ideological reasons'.[2] In 1998, the Israeli government approved a plan that defined 553 towns and villages as NPAs: four of them were Arab (less than 1 per cent).[3]

After a legal battle, Israel's High Court ruled in 2006 that the NPA decision was discriminatory.[4] Unsurprisingly, this angered many, like Sderot mayor Eli Moyal, who said it was not shameful for the state to 'prefer Jews because this is the state of the Jews'. Shmuel Rifman, head of the Ramat Negev Regional Council, commented: 'There are criteria, maybe the court doesn't like them, but there are. The government wants to encourage Jews to move to the Negev and Galilee and to encourage those already living there to stay there.'

In 2009, the state sought to get around this problem through a section in the new Economy Efficiency Law that 'grants the government sweeping discretion to classify towns, villages and areas as NPAs and to allocate enormous state resources without criteria'.[5] Then in December, a new NPA map was issued which, the Prime Minister's Office claimed, encompassed almost two million Israelis, 40 per cent of whom were Palestinian citizens.[6] Yet rather than being a positive step forward, under the new rules, a town in an NPA region does not automatically receive benefits, but are dependent on the 'exclusive discretion' of 'individual ministers'. The potential for continued discrimination, then, remains, perhaps even worsened by a further degree of unaccountability.[7] The exception to this is Jewish settlements in the West Bank, which each receive the 'associated additional budgetary grants'.

THE GAP

The gap between Jewish and Palestinian citizens, in terms of the statistics for the likes of quality of life and employment prospects, is a further indicator of the discrimination faced by the state's minority. In 2003, close to half of all Palestinian families lived in poverty compared to around one in five Jewish Israeli families.[8] In 2010, Palestinian citizens accounted for a third of all poor people in Israel.[9] Out of the 30 communities in Israel with the most unemployment, 27 of them are Arab.[10] In

2002, government statistics grouped over 200 villages, towns, and cities into ten 'clusters' according to socioeconomic factors. In the lowest ranked cluster, nine out of ten communities were Palestinian. Arab localities made up 83 per cent of localities in the lowest three clusters combined.[11]

With a higher unemployment rate and an average income per Palestinian family 63 per cent that of the average Jewish family, it is not surprising that even more fundamental indicators highlight the disparity.[12] The 2008 figures for life expectancy show that a male Jew can expect to live more than three years longer than a Palestinian citizen, while the gap for women is four years.[13]

Another significant problem facing the Palestinian minority is the discriminatory system of budget allocations and benefits (beyond those outlined as part of the National Priority Areas designation). Strikingly, even though there are 'three times as many Arab families under the poverty line as Jewish families', the state spends on average 35 per cent more on each Jewish citizen than Palestinian citizens.[14] An additional means of providing benefits to primarily Jewish citizens has been 'compensating persons who serve in the security forces'.[15]

In 2004, only 4 per cent of the development budget was earmarked for the Palestinian community.[16] Other studies show that 'the average sum budgeted per capita in the Arab municipal budgets is 25–30 per cent of that of the Jewish municipal budgets'.[17] Such a gaping disparity between state resources and the size and needs of the minority is not bettered by suggesting that many Palestinians live in so-called 'mixed cities' (e.g. Haifa, Acre), which in fact only account for around 9 per cent of the entire Arab community.[18]

In addition, Palestinian citizens face severe challenges in the job market, where they encounter discrimination and whole sectors effectively off limits. At the end of 2009, the number of Palestinian state employees stood at 6.6 per cent of the total – excluding the health system this falls to 5.2 per cent.[19] Moreover, 'no more than eight Arabs are contractually employed in a senior position'. In 2003, there were no Palestinians in the Ministry of Communications, and two in the Ministry of

National Infrastructure.[20] In 2010, a report revealed that from thousands of government employees in the Negev, only 16 of them are non-Jewish (in a region where 25 per cent of the population is Bedouin).[21]

This kind of reality is mirrored in much of the private sector. In 2005, only 9 per cent of directors of public corporations were Palestinian, while communications giant Bezeq employs less than a dozen Palestinian citizens from a 10,000-strong workforce.[22] In 2011, government data showed that of the over 2.3 million people employed by 170,000 Jewish-owned businesses, less than 86,000 – around 3.7 per cent – are Palestinian citizens.[23] A 2010 survey of almost 200 industrial firms found that 41 per cent did not 'employ any Arab college graduates'.[24]

In the last couple of years, there has been a concerted effort by both the Israeli government and private sector to talk up the economic potential of the Arab community, with conferences, proposed investment initiatives, and talk of Israeli businesses 'waking up' to the Palestinian minority.[25] Yet the reason why the 'Israeli Arab sector' has become an issue of concern seems to be because of a realisation, in the words of the director of the Economic Development Authority in the Minority Sector, that 'if Israel wants to attain economic growth of 6% to 7%, it must allocate budgets to close the economic disparities'.[26]

Seeing the national economic potential in 'equalizing the income' of Jews and Palestinian citizens is what motivates this focus, not a sudden desire to address the symptoms, let alone the roots, of systematic discrimination. There is also the context of Israel's successful bid to become a member of the Organization for Economic Cooperation and Development (OECD), who stressed the importance of 'developing' the 'Arab sector' when admitting Israel.[27] There is even an echo of the pre-1966 military regime's 'carrot and stick' approach when industrialist Stef Wertheimer describes 'the industrial park in Arab Nazareth' as a 'good example of coexistence': 'When people work together, they have no time for nonsense. They're too tired at night to commit terrorist acts. They're satisfied, they engage in producing. They work together, not against each other.'[28]

EDUCATION

In Israel, Jewish and Palestinian citizens are educated in separate, parallel systems. Palestinian children are not legally prevented from attending Jewish schools; it is a consequence of an enrollment system based on residence, plus little support in either community for mixing.[29] Successive Israeli governments have fostered a profound divide in the two groups' education systems, through discriminatory funding and budgeting – a state of affairs that makes an important contribution to fundamental inequalities between the two communities in general.

In a study conducted in association with the Israeli Central Bureau of Statistics, it was found that for each Jewish student, schools have a budget of around US$1,100 a year. For each Palestinian child, however, the figure was just US$191: almost six times smaller.[30] In the south of Israel, the research showed there was US$60 for each Palestinian student – while for children of West Bank settlers, the budget was US$1,535.

The impact of the discriminatory funding is felt across the board, in terms of facilities, teaching quality, and class sizes. For example, in elementary school, the average number of students per classroom is 18 per cent higher in Palestinian schools.[31] Moreover, despite the fact that Palestinian citizens are more likely to come from an underprivileged background, 'the average per-student allocation in Arab junior high schools amounts to only 20 per cent of the average in Jewish junior highs'.[32]

The inequality in education is not a secret – a former senior official of the Education Ministry has said that the large gap created between Jewish and Palestinian education will be very difficult to close.[33] This is because of the scale of separation, which is 'manifested in the educational goals of the two systems, in their curricula, in their budgets and facilities, in the rates of success of their students, and in the occupational opportunities open to their graduates'.[34]

In 2001, Human Rights Watch produced a report on the discrimination faced by Palestinian children in Israel's schools.

> Their schools are a world apart in quality from the public schools serving Israel's majority Jewish population. Often overcrowded and understaffed, poorly built, badly maintained, or simply unavailable, schools for Palestinian Arab children offer fewer facilities and educational opportunities than are offered other Israeli children.[35]

The conclusion was damning: 'Discrimination against Palestinian Arab children colors every aspect of the two systems.'

The inequalities in schooling then impact on Palestinians' opportunities in higher education, which in turn has a knock on effect for job prospects and the economic health of the community as a whole. This systematic discrimination in questions of budgets, employment, and education cannot be seen in isolation from the rest of the regime, which serves to perpetuate Palestinian citizens' inferior position as a colonised minority.

5
Frustrating Democratic Change

Since 1948, Israeli authorities have been sure to define the space 'allowed' for dissent and radical change, an opportunity particularly restricted for Palestinian citizens. In this chapter, we will look at how efforts to peacefully contest the structure of Jewish privilege have been thwarted and criminalised: from the twelve-year-old boy in the 1950s answering to a military governor for a poem, to the contemporary Shin Bet's declared objective of targeting Palestinian citizens who, within the democratic means afforded to them, challenge the nature of Israel as a 'Jewish democracy'.

MILITARY RULE

> The [military] regime ... set out to maintain the social segregation of Arabs and Jews, to extract certain important resources from the Arab population, and to regulate and direct the behaviour of the Arab minority to serve the interests of the Jewish majority.[1]

In the new Israeli state, Palestinian citizens were placed under a military regime that would shape the community for a generation. Ironically, the man who went on to become Israel's Minister of Justice, Dov Yosef, had described the British Emergency Defense Regulations – the basis for Israel's military regime – as 'terrorism under official seal'.[2] The formal end to the military regime only came in 1966, meaning it had lasted an entire generation post-Nakba. Over the years, different elements had been phased out, though almost a decade after the establishment of the state, 80–90 per cent of Palestinian citizens still lived under military rule.[3]

Yehoshua Palmon served as the Israeli Prime Minister's first adviser on Arab affairs, a role that put him 'in charge of liaison between the Military Governor and the government Ministries, as well as the coordination of martial rule'.[4] He would later describe the government's policy towards the Palestinian citizens as having been one of 'separate development', done, he said, in order to 'maintain a democratic regime within the Jewish population alone'. A subsequent Arab affairs adviser, Uri Lubrani, put it like this: 'We give them tractors, electricity, and progress, but we take land and restrict their movement ... if they [Arabs] would remain hewers of wood perhaps it would be easier to control them.'[5]

One important use of the military regime by the Israeli authorities was to 'expel' or 'relocate' groups of Palestinian citizens, especially in the Negev and border villages.[6] At least 2,000 Palestinians were 'transferred' to Gaza in 1950, while according to a Foreign Ministry report, during 1949–53 Israel expelled almost 17,000 Bedouin Palestinians from the Negev.[7] Then there was Article 125 of the Defense (Emergency) Regulations (see Chapter 2) which allowed for 'the closing of any area for security purposes' as well as the expulsion 'of its inhabitants'.[8] Thus, subordinating Palestinian citizens to these military regulations was 'aimed at furthering Zionist goals and consolidating the construction of Israel as a Jewish state'.[9]

One of the most onerous and restrictive aspects of the military regime – echoed today in the Occupied West Bank – was the travel permit system. This control over Palestinians' freedom of movement included the requirement 'to carry means of identification and travel permits, at all times' and 'buses were frequently stopped on the roads' to take off 'Arab passengers' and 'verify their permits'.[10]

Over one nine-month period in 1951, over 2,000 Palestinian citizens were tried by military courts, most of them 'for crossing in or out of closed areas without a permit'.[11] These restrictions were incrementally relaxed, yet in 1958 only one in three Palestinians in the 'military zones at any given time held travel permits'.[12] Even by 1964, 'key restrictions still remained'. The

PM's second adviser on Arab affairs, Samuel Divon, once asked, 'Consider what would happen if we abolished the restrictions.

> The Arabs who used to live in the empty villages ... would go back and squat on their ruins, demanding their lands back ... And then, when they have made as much trouble as possible about their own lands, they will start clamouring for the return of the refugees.[13]

The ability to repress Palestinian dissent was a key benefit of the military regime, from the point of view of the Israeli political-security establishment. Indeed, former general and then-Member of Knesset Yigal Allon argued in favour of the military administration in 1959 on the grounds that it provided 'a legal basis for actions taken against treasonous assemblies and so that traitors can be punished', as well as 'a basis to prevent and deter hostile political actions and organisations'.[14]

The steps taken against these Palestinian 'traitors' were draconian. Shmuel Divon described the approach taken towards opposition:

> Ben-Gurion always reminds us that we cannot be guided by subversion which the Arab minority has not engaged in. We must be guided by what they might have done if they had been given the chance.[15]

Palestinian political activists 'were often exiled from their villages or placed under administrative detention', and 'entire villages' could be punished by, for example, having requests for improved infrastructure refused.[16] Even children were not exempt: as a twelve-year-old boy, Palestinian poet Mahmoud Darwish was summoned by the military governor after performing a poem that 'reflected on our situation as Arabs forced to celebrate Israel's Independence Day'.[17] Meanwhile, the necessary 'proper political behaviour' helped to gain 'rights' like work and travel.[18]

Additionally, Palestinian citizens under the military administration were tried before military tribunals many of whose decisions 'could not be appealed to the civilian court system'.[19] The military court judge was also not required 'to explain the use of the term "security considerations" as a justification for suspicion, punishment, or procedure'.[20] One regulation used by the regime 'made it possible to place a person under administrative arrest for an unlimited time, without explanation and without trial'.[21]

As part of this control of the Palestinian minority, the Israeli security forces 'quickly created networks of informers and collaborators'.[22] One of the tasks of such informers was to 'keep a special eye on schoolteachers', part of a 'comprehensive system of reports' delivered back to the authorities.[23] Recently, it was revealed that the secret service even sent undercover spies to live in Palestinian villages, marrying and having families.[24]

Along with a system of monitoring and reward/punishment, frustrating democracy was high on the list of priorities, a policy legitimised by dismissing 'existing conditions in the Arab community' as unsuitable for democratic elections.[25] In 1953, Arab affairs adviser Yehoshua Palmon put it like this: 'In the Arab community one must choose a "middle road" of not-too-much democracy'.[26] Once they were allowed, local village council elections were manipulated by the security agencies in order to ensure 'that "their" Arabs received positions of power'.[27] Furthermore, there was a deliberate attempt to encourage the fragmentation of Palestinians along sectarian lines, 'exacerbate[ing] distinctions and discord', and 'play[ing] off one religious and ethnic community against another'.[28]

> The political aims of the martial rule in the early years of its existence were summed up in the following words, contained in a top secret memorandum: 'The government's policy ... has sought to divide the Arab population into diverse communities and regions.'[29]

As part of Israel's wider regime of control, a key goal of the military administration was to 'reshape Arab consciousness and identity' in order to create 'this new Israeli Arab identity'.[30]

> By reporting on the day-to-day speech of Arabs and by summoning and interrogating those Arabs who spoke against the state, the security authorities 'taught' the minority what was fit to be said and what was unacceptable, thus shaping the contours of Arab political discourse in Israel.[31]

FRUSTRATING DEMOCRATIC CHANGE

This suppression of dissent has continued after the end of the military regime in 1966, right up to the present day. The infamous 1976 Koenig memorandum, mentioned in Chapter 3 in the context of Judaisation, advocated the adoption of 'tough measurers at all levels against various agitators among college and university students'.[32] In 1980, Professor Ian Lustick described how the Office of the Adviser to the Prime Minister on Arab Affairs would suggest to universities that Palestinian student committees 'constitute[d] threats to the security of the state' and infiltrate 'student groups with informants and provocateurs'.[33] In the First Intifada, 'Palestinian and joint Palestinan-Jewish student organizations were constrained, and students who were active against the occupation were severely punished by their universities'.[34]

In 1998, the then Prime Minister, Benjamin Netanyahu, held discussions on the 'growing Palestinianization and religious radicalization among Israel's Arabs'. Participants in one session 'included the pertinent ministers, the head of the Shin Bet, and other security bodies'.[35] A decade on, and Shin Bet head Yuval Diskin told US officials that many Palestinian citizens 'take their rights too far'.[36]

In 2007, the Prime Minister's Office revealed that the Shin Bet security service would 'thwart the activity of any group or individual seeking to harm the Jewish and democratic character of the State of Israel, even if such activity is sanctioned by the law'.[37] Shortly after, Shin Bet emphasised that it goes after 'individuals deemed as "conducting subversive activity against the Jewish identity of the state," even if their actions are not in violation of the law'.[38] Israel's attorney general wrote that the letter was written 'in coordination' with him and 'with his agreement'.[39]

An example of what this means in practice is the arrest, trial, and sentencing of Ameer Makhoul. In May 2010, Makhoul, director of the Arab NGO network Ittijah, was snatched from his house in the night, and for almost two weeks, prevented from meeting his lawyers. Subjected to 'interrogation' methods that included sleep deprivation and being kept shackled to a chair, a 'confession' Makhoul described as coerced was ultimately used to convict him of espionage for Hezbollah. In January 2009, Makhoul had been told by a Shin Bet agent that 'next time' he would 'have to say goodbye to his family since he will leave them for a long time'.[40] After Makhoul received a nine year sentence, Amnesty International responded:

> Ameer Makhoul is well known for his human rights activism on behalf of Palestinians in Israel and those living under Israeli occupation. We fear that this may be the underlying reason for his imprisonment.[41]

The targeting of Makhoul comes at a time when the space in Israel for dissent is shrinking. In March 2011, the Knesset passed a law enabling the withholding of public funds to local authorities and other bodies who mark the Nakba or who are 'deemed to be involved in publicly challenging the founding of

Photograph 6 Janan Abdu holding a photograph of her jailed husband, Ameer Makhoul. (July 2010, Ben White)

Israel as a Jewish state'.[42] An editorial in *Ha'aretz* wrote that 'in essence, this is a law designed to shut people up'.[43]

One of the bill's supporters, MK Alex Miller, described teaching the expulsion and dispossession of Palestinians in 1948 (the Nakba) in Israeli schools as 'incitement', and linked it to 'an issue of how a citizen defines his citizenship in the state where he lives'.[44] By that stage, the Education Minister, Gideon Sa'ar, had already banned school textbooks from mentioning the Nakba, creating an environment where teachers who used unofficial materials to discuss the topic are afraid to use their real names in press reports.[45]

Palestinian members of the Knesset are also increasingly under attack, with challenges to their parliamentary immunity

Janan Abdu

Janan Abdu is a social and feminist activist and researcher. She is married to Palestinian political prisoner Ameer Makhoul.

'The date of 6 May 2010 is forever etched in our memory, the day after which all of our lives changed. After the security forces took Ameer, for almost two weeks there was no meetings with a lawyer – we didn't know anything about his circumstances. Since the arrest we meet once every two weeks from behind a glass screen and talk with him through the handset. Ameer cannot hug or kiss his children.

'My daughters live everyday life without the presence of their father – it's hard. When my oldest daughter finished school, Ameer was not at her graduation ceremony, and our youngest daughter will leave school in five years, also without her dad. These things hurt a lot. We all miss him every day, but he still lives with us in every moment. We are patient, and we resist. Our daughter Hind, now 18, wrote him a letter saying, "Resistance needs to come from anger, not sadness or pity, to continue and succeed". Our youngest daughter Huda, 14 years old, wrote to Ameer: "We are steadfast if we are young or old, happy or sad, free or in prison, together or separated. We will remain steadfast".'

Source: Interview with author.

and their very presence in the parliament questioned.[46] MK Haneen Zoabi (author of this book's foreword) has been the focus more than others, on account of her outspoken defence of Palestinian rights, and participation in initiatives such as the Freedom Flotilla.

Across Israel, Zoabi has been the object of hate: Netanya's mayor supported her expulsion from the country, while a Facebook group calling for her murder quickly gained hundreds of members. Zoabi was almost physically assaulted in the chamber, as she faced cries of 'Go to Gaza, traitor'.[47] Other Palestinian members of the Knesset received an e-mail from MK Michael Ben-Ari announcing that 'after we deal with her [Zoabi], it will be your turn'.[48]

Post-flotilla, the Knesset voted to revoke some of Zoabi's parliamentary privileges. During the debate preceding the vote, the head of the House Committee MK Yariv Levin told Zoabi: 'You don't belong in the Israeli Knesset, you don't deserve to hold an Israeli ID card. You're an embarrassment to the citizens of Israel, to the Arab community, and to your family.'[49]

The committee that Levin chairs is responsible, among other things, for dealing with requests to lift immunity from MKs. In February 2010, Levin expressed his belief that 'a serious decision' must be made about 'whether or not these parties [Arab MKs] can continue to sit in the Israeli parliament, even while they operate against the country'.[50]

BRUTALITY AND IMPUNITY

Palestinian citizens must also contend with a police force and justice system that treats Arabs different to Jews, a context where extreme violence is meted out to Palestinians by security forces with impunity. In 2001, an Amnesty International report stated that 'prejudice against Palestinian citizens of Israel is widespread in the criminal justice system, both in the courts and law enforcement methods'.[51] This was highlighted by a judge in 2009 who, while acquitting an accused Palestinian teenager, 'accepted the defense counsel's claim that the State engages in a discriminatory policy against Arab youth involved in offenses of "ideological violence"'.[52]

There is a long history of a lack of accountability for state forces that carry out violence against Palestinian citizens, going back to the Kafr Qasim massacre in 1956 when close to 50 villagers were murdered by soldiers enforcing a curfew. The eight soldiers who received jail terms had their sentences commuted, and were all out four years later. The commanding officer was fined an agora, 'Israel's smallest coin'.[53] Twenty years later, when Israeli forces shot dead six Palestinian citizens on Land Day, Yitzhak Rabin's cabinet 'unanimously commended the security forces for their 'restraint' in handling the strike and the ensuing disturbances'.[54]

A more recent defining moment was the killing of 13 Palestinian citizens by Israeli police in October 2000, during protests in solidarity with the uprising of the Palestinians in the occupied territories. Even though the official commission found that sniper fire was responsible for the deaths and injuries of citizens, no one has ever been prosecuted for these deaths.[55] Despite the fact that there was also large scale, violent riots by Jewish Israelis, the only fatalities were Palestinian. In a 2001 report, Amnesty International cited a border policewoman who had testified before the investigating commission, who told a journalist: 'We handle Jewish riots differently. When such a demonstration takes place, it is obvious from the start that we do not bring our guns along. These are our instructions.'[56]

This kind of discrimination was manifested in the wider crackdown at the start of the Second Intifada. From the roughly 1,000 Israeli citizens arrested between 28 September and 30 October, around 66 per cent were Palestinian and 34 per cent Jewish.[57] Yet of those detained until the end of their trial, 89 per cent were Palestinian citizens. In January 2009, during Israel's assault on the Gaza Strip, over 800 Israeli citizens, the vast majority Palestinian, were arrested during protests. A third of detainees were under 18 years old, and 86 per cent of these minors were kept in custody until the end of proceedings.[58]

Thus it is not enough that Palestinians in Israel are second-class citizens subject to discriminatory land, housing, and economic policies: if they resist apartheid, express solidarity with their fellow Palestinians under military rule, or work towards a state of all its citizens, they experience the heavy hand of the state. Change from within the current system has not come, and will not do so: there must be a new way, and a different future.

6
Rethink to Reimagine

An examination of Israel's policies of segregation and ethno-national discrimination towards its Palestinian minority is instructive because they have Israeli citizenship. Despite the substantial evidence to the contrary, it is possible for the Israeli government to deflect attention from its apartheid regime in the West Bank by citing 'security' concerns and describing the territory as 'disputed'. If there are different rights for the settlers in Ariel compared to Palestinians in Nablus, so this line goes, that's because the former are citizens and the latter are subject to a mixture of Israeli military law and Palestinian Authority jurisdiction.

The Palestinians of Nazareth, al-Araqib, and Lod, however, are citizens in a polity that not only presents itself as a democracy, but boasts of the rights it says are afforded to non-Jews. When Israel looks to refute charges of 'apartheid' or systematic racism, it points to examples of 'Arab Israeli' Knesset members, judges, and pop stars. Israel's lobbyists remind us that in Israel, 'Arabs and Jews' share the same beaches, work in the same hospitals, etc.

But when you consider these facts alongside the best part of 70 years of state-sponsored racial discrimination with regards to land, housing, and citizenship, then parading (the few) examples of Palestinian public figures is, at best, a grand exercise in missing the point. The truth is that policies which would be considered grotesquely racist applied in other contexts are routine and institutionalized in Israel.

Increasingly, links are being made between the experience of non-Jewish citizens in the 'Jewish and democratic' state, and Palestinians living under Israeli occupation in the West Bank and Gaza. This is inevitable: at the same time as bulldozers tear down 'illegal' homes in the Jordan Valley, al-Araqib is destroyed and its residents described as 'trespassers'. The same priorities are at work in the Galilee and the hills of 'Judea and Samaria': break up Palestinian territorial contiguity, further Jewish settlement, and ensure the maintenance of a regime of control that benefits one group at the expense of another.

Photograph 7 Arafat Ismayil, head of the Dahmash village committee, an unrecognised Palestinian community threatened with demolition. (July 2010, Ben White)

As Professor Oren Yiftachel has put it, 'the colonized West Bank, the besieged Gaza Strip and Israel proper, each with its own official set of rules' are 'merging into one regime system, ultimately controlled by the Jewish state'.[1] Yiftachel likens the situation to apartheid, with people granted 'citizenship status akin to "blacks", "coloreds" and "whites"'. In this de facto one state, the Palestinians are divided into different groups 'each having a differently inferior set of rights and capabilities'.

By the mid 1990s, the expansionist drive in the occupied Palestinian territories was largely exhausted, and the focus turned towards 'consolidation', developing and fine-tuning 'a system of rule that aims to cement separate and unequal ethnic relations'.[2] Concurrently, 'the gaze turn[ed] inwards, to the "unfinished" war of 1948' – that is to say, the 'demographic threat' – and the project of Judaising the Galilee and Negev.[3]

Photograph 8 Demolished Palestinian structure in the Jordan Valley region of the West Bank. (July 2010, Ben White)

There is an urgent need to rethink our approach to Israel, consistent with the reality on the ground in the West Bank, the reasons for the failure of the 'peace process', and the situation for the Palestinian minority in a Jewish state. It means moving beyond the 'occupation' discourse that limits the conflict to policies and phenomena specific to the territories conquered by Israel in 1967. It is time to re-integrate the different elements

Map 4 Access 2011 (left to right) Israeli ID, West Bank ID, Gaza ID, stateless Palestinian refugee. (arenaofspeculation.org)

Map 5 Jewish-owned land 1918, 1947, Israeli 'state land' 1960, 2008. (arenaofspeculation.org, based on Malkit Shoshan, B'Tselem)

of the historic conflict, and see the 'Question of Palestine' holistically.

Part of this rethinking has to involve questioning the orthodoxy about Israel's democratic credentials, an alternative analysis that is rooted in the cold, hard facts of expulsion, land confiscation, and unequal concepts of citizenship and nationality. But if Israel is not a democracy, what is it? There is perhaps no one adequate framework. Apartheid, settler-colonialism, xenophobia – they are all useful in different ways, but the description is still lacking. It is a kind of politics of ethnic purity, where ethnic survival is a supreme value, and Palestinians – indigenous to the land – become an intrinsic security threat.

The appropriate way to identify such a framework is not to focus purely on the condition of Palestinians with Israeli citizenship. Rather, it is necessary to see how, as a result of Israeli policies and legislation, one in seven Palestinians is a second-class citizen, a third are under military rule without citizenship, and half of all Palestinians are outside the borders, dispossessed and forbidden from returning. This latter reality is central to the contradiction of the 'Jewish and democratic' state, an identification that was only established, and can only be maintained, by the expulsion and forcible exclusion of half the Palestinian people.

The increased focus by Israel and its lobbyists in the West on the threat posed by so-called 'delegitimisation' is revealing. As the calls for Palestinian basic rights to be implemented grow louder, so does the frantic attempts to fence-off debate about Israel's 'right' to be a Jewish state. The efforts to equate anti-Zionism with antisemitism are a sign that the conflict's core issues are being exposed – and that's got the defenders of Jewish privilege in Palestine/Israel worried.

Given that the Israeli state since 1948 has been a regime intended to 'ensure the homogeneity of Jewish national identity over the territorial spatial sphere, free from Palestinians with a collective identity', it is unsurprising that in the policies towards Palestinian citizens we find ultimate proof that 'such a regime cannot possibly be democratic'.[4]

> [The Palestinians in Israel] serve as a constant reminder of the skeleton [the regime] keeps in the closet: the ethnic cleansing of Palestine in 1948 – the expulsion, the expropriation of land, the obliteration of towns and villages, and the inaccuracy of the historiographic narrative aimed at justifying all these actions. The fact that the cleansing of the Jewish sovereign territory – achieved by expelling Palestinians, by frightening them, and by forcing them to flee – remains incomplete leaves the ongoing presence of Palestinians in Israel as profound testimony to the undemocratic nature of Israeli sovereignty.

This is what we need: an analysis free from 'peace process' clichés and tired Zionist-pushed talking points, an understanding shaped by the relentless colonisation of Palestine (the famous 'facts on the ground'). But that is obviously not enough. Rethinking must lead to reimagining: reimagining the Jewish and Palestinian presence in Palestine/Israel, and a future based on a genuine co-existence of equals, rather than ethno-religious supremacy and segregation.

It is fascinating that at the same time as the Zionist project in Palestine reaches an impasse, across the Middle East popular uprisings are undermining the status quo and forcing old assumptions to be rethought or rejected. Writing in February 2011, I described what I called the 'liberation of the imagination' where people living under oppression realise that contrary to the regime's propaganda, their situation is not eternal and the power of the dictator and his security apparatus is not infinite.[5] Palestinian political prisoner Ameer Makhoul, in a piece penned in jail, wrote: 'For in a dictatorship, everything goes well until the last 15 minutes.'[6]

Forget the simplistic dismissal that the revolts from Tunisia to Yemen have 'nothing to do with Israel': the links between the Arab uprisings and the Palestinians' (ongoing) revolution are profound. The Palestinian struggle has inspired the Middle East, and certainly in the case of Egypt, protests in solidarity with the Second Intifada were a key part in a decade of growing dissent prior to the toppling of Mubarak. It's not about causation: Tunisians rejected Ben Ali for their own good reasons. It's about the threat of a good example: the way the Palestinians have embodied a fight for dignity and basic rights without surrender.

Now we are seeing the spirit of *intifada* (literally 'shaking off') that emerged from Tunisia and spread to Egypt helping to inspire a new, revitalisation of the Palestinian revolution. It is impossible, writing this, to predict what will have happened even by the time you are reading this – let alone further into the future. But the Nakba Day protests of May 2011 showed that a sense of empowerment and initiative has returned to the Palestinian struggle for justice, feeding off the visible strength and potential of people power demonstrated across the region.

The question then, is can this liberation of the imagination extend to Palestine/Israel, and what will that look like? In *One Country*, Ali Abunimah quotes Israeli author Daniel Gavron, who concluded in his book 'The other side of despair' that 'the territory between the Mediterranean and the Jordan River must be shared but cannot be sensibly partitioned.' The 'only one alternative' left? 'Israeli-Palestinian coexistence in one nation'.[7]

Seeing all of Palestine/Israel as one 'unit' is not just a way of understanding the last seven decades of Zionist colonisation and the emergence of an apartheid regime of control. It is also the basis for a future solution that protects the rights of both the Palestinian people and Jewish Israelis, a 'redefining' of self-determination that means both groups share a common homeland 'based on full group and individual equality'.[8]

One of the important aspects of the Boycott Divestment Sanctions (BDS) campaign is the way in which the three simple demands, that are the foundation of this Palestinian call for global civil society solidarity, are focused on rights:

- The right of Palestinians to be free from military rule in the post-1967 occupied territories.
- The right of Palestinian citizens of Israel to full equality.
- The rights of Palestinian refugees to return and reparations.[9]

This emphasis on rights and equality, like Israeli academic Amnon Raz-Krakotzkin's approach to 'the concept of bi-nationalism', does not so much 'describe a "solution"', but rather serves 'as a crucial point of departure and perspective to direct the struggle towards democratization and de-colonization, based upon the recognition of both Palestinian and Jewish rights'.[10]

Freed from the imperative of maintaining an exclusivist ethno-religious state, issues like water rights or the status of Jerusalem are transformed from the stumbling blocks of tortuous negotiations into opportunities for celebratory affirmations of a common homeland and the mutual protection of both communities' rights. This kind of new perspective means that 'instead of asking "can we return?" or "when will we return?"', Palestinian refugees can ask 'what kind of return do we want to create for ourselves?'[11]

There is a good deal standing in the way of realising a future where Jewish Israelis and Palestinians share the land as equals. There are a few who make substantial profits from the existing regime, while others are paralysed by apathy or fear. The Palestinian people know from decades of experience that even the smallest gains in their struggle for liberation are not achieved without a fight or a cost.

But there is surely no other option. Many people are familiar with the words of Israeli military chief of staff Moshe Dayan at a funeral in 1956, when he reminded those present that Palestinian refugees in Gaza had been watching the transformation of 'the lands and the villages, where they and their fathers dwelt, into our estate'. Less well known are the thoughts of his father, MK Shmuel Dayan, who in 1950 admitted: 'Maybe [not allowing the refugees back] is not right and not moral, but if we become just and moral, I do not know where we will end up.'[12]

An answer to Dayan's question that resounds with defiant hope, rather than fear and privilege, comes from the Palestinians and Jewish Israelis – as well as many around the world of all backgrounds – who understand, in the words of Edward Said, that 'coexistence, sharing, [and] community must win out over exclusivism, intransigence, and rejectionism'.[13] There is no time to waste.

Appendix
Ten Facts About Palestinian Citizens in Israel

1. Since 1948, over 700 Jewish communities have been established in Israel (not including settlements in the occupied territories). The only towns established for Palestinian citizens were seven in the Negev, and only as a way of removing the Bedouin population from other areas.
2. Significant authority over areas like land ownership and rural settlement is invested in bodies that are constitutionally-mandated to privilege Jews.
3. The amount of land belonging to Palestinian refugees that was expropriated by Israel's 'Absentee Property Law' amounts to around 20 per cent of the country's total pre-1967 territory.
4. Roughly one in four Palestinian citizens are 'present absentees' (i.e. internally displaced), their lands and property confiscated by the state.
5. An estimated 90,000 Palestinian citizens live in dozens of 'unrecognised villages' in Israel. They suffer from home demolitions and a lack of basic infrastructure.
6. Residency in 70 per cent of Israeli towns is controlled by admissions committees that filter out those deemed 'unsuitable' for the 'social fabric' of the community.
7. Despite making up 20 per cent of the population, the state development budget for the Palestinian minority is just 4 per cent.
8. The Education Ministry spends more than five times as much on Jewish students as Palestinian students.

9. Public officials, including Members of Knesset and cabinet members, routinely and publicly express racism towards Palestinians with impunity.
10. Shin Bet, the domestic intelligence agency/secret police, openly fights peaceful and legal efforts by Palestinian citizens to challenge the 'Jewish' nature of the state.

Notes

INTRODUCTION

1. Tawfiq Zayyad, 'Here We Shall Stay', in Salma Khadra Jayyusi (ed.), *Anthology of Modern Palestinian Literature*, New York: Columbia University Press, 1992, pp.327–8.
2. Arthur Hertzberg, *The Zionist Idea*, Philadelphia: The Jewish Publication Society, 1997, p.222.
3. Hillel Cohen, *Good Arabs*, Berkeley: University of California Press, 2010, p.233.
4. Ben White, 'Netanyahu: Erasing the Green Line', *Al Jazeera*, 27 April 2010.
5. Ben White, 'The political fading of the Green Line', *Middle East International*, 5 March 2010.
6. Nadim N. Rouhana and Nimer Sultanty, 'Redrawing the Boundaries of Citizenship: Israel's New Hegemony', *Journal of Palestine Studies*, Vol. 33, No. 1. (Autumn, 2003), 5–22.
7. '2008 Sikkuy report: huge socioeconomic gap between Jews and Arabs (with this government, it's likely to grow)', Promised Land blog, www.promisedlandblog.com/?p=1885 (last accessed 21 June 2011).
8. Hertzberg, *The Zionist Idea*, p.245.
9. Anton La Guardia, *Holy Land Unholy War*, London: John Murray, 2002, p.77.
10. Zeev Sternhell, *The Founding Myths of Israel: Nationalism, Socialism, and the Making of the Jewish State*, Princeton, NJ: Princeton University Press, pp.71–2.
11. Ian Lustick, *Arabs in the Jewish State*, Austin, TX: University of Texas Press, 1980, pp.34–5.
12. Michael Makovsky, *Churchill's Promised Land: Zionism and Statecraft*, New Haven, CT: Yale University Press, p.156.

13. Victor Kattan, 'The Failure to Establish Democracy in Palestine: From the British Mandate to the Present times', *Jadaliyya*, 2 April 2011.
14. Nur Masalha, *Expulsion of the Palestinians*, Washington DC: Institute for Palestine Studies, 2001, p.6.
15. Ronald Storrs, *The Memoirs of Sir Ronald Storrs*, Pittstown, NJ: Arno Press, p.396.
16. Tom Segev, *One Palestine, Complete*, London: Abacus, 2002, p.119.
17. Evan M. Wilson, *A Calculated Risk: The U.S. Decision to Recognize Israel*, Cincinnati, OH: Clerisy Press, 2008, pp.228, 234.
18. See, for example, Ilan Pappe, *The Ethnic Cleansing of Palestine*, Oxford: Oneworld Publications, 2007.

CHAPTER 1. 'JEWISH *AND* DEMOCRATIC'?

1. 'Will the real Shimon Peres please stand up?' *Ha'aretz*, 8 May 2011.
2. Oren Yiftachel, *Ethnocracy: Land and Identity Politics in Israel/Palestine*, Philadelphia: University of Pennsylvania Press, 2006, p.84.
3. Haim Misgav, 'This is not racism', *Ynetnews.com*, 9 October 2009.
4. Eliezer Schweid, 'Israel as a Zionist state', *World Zionist Organization*, www.doingzionism.org/resources/view.asp?id=1365 (last accessed 21 June 2011).
5. Baruch Kimmerling, 'Boundaries and frontiers of the Israeli control system: analytical conclusions', in Baruch Kimmerling (ed.), *The Israeli State and Society: Boundaries and Frontiers*, Albany, NY: State University of New York Press, 1989, pp.265–84 (274).
6. *Ha'aretz*, 28 August 2002.
7. Yifat Holzman-Gazit, *Land Expropriation in Israel: Law, Culture and Society*, Aldershot: Ashgate, 2007, p.102.
8. Ruth Gavison, 'The Jews' right to statehood: a defense', *Azure*, Summer 5763/2003, no. 15.

9. Charles S. Liebman and Eliezer Don-Yehiya, *Civil Religion in Israel: Traditional Judaism and Political Culture in the Jewish State*, Berkeley, CA: University of California Press, 1983, p.12.
10. Uri Davis, *Apartheid Israel*, London: Zed Books, 2003, p.70.
11. Jewish Agency for Israel website, www.jewishagency.org/JewishAgency/English/Aliyah/Aliyah+Info/The+Law+of+Return (last accessed 21 June 2011).
12. Dina Siegel, *The Great Immigration: Russian Jews in Israel*, New York: Berghahn Books, 1998, p.9.
13. 'Analysis: What kind of aliya is best to ensure the survival of the Jewish people?' *Jerusalem Post*, 1 January 2007.
14. www.israellawresourcecenter.org/israellaws/fulltext/nationalitylaw.htm (last accessed 21 June 2011).
15. United Nations General Assembly Resolution 181, November 29, 1947, www.yale.edu/lawweb/avalon/un/res181.htm (last accessed 21 June 2011).
16. www.un.org/en/documents/udhr/index.shtml (last accessed 21 June 2011).
17. Roselle Tekiner, 'The "Who is a Jew" controversy in Israel: a produce of political Zionism', in Roselle Tekiner, Samir Abed-Rabbo and Norton Mezvinsky (eds), *Anti-Zionism: Analytical Reflections*, Brattleboro, VT: Amana Books, 1988, pp.62–89 (70).
18. Virginia Tilley, *The One-State Solution*, Michigan: University of Michigan Press, 2005, p.147.
19. David Kretzmer, *The Legal Status of the Arabs in Israel*, Boulder, CO: Westview Press, 1990, p.44.
20. 'Report of the Special Rapporteur on adequate housing as a component of the right to an adequate standard of living, Mr. Miloon Kothari', UN Commission on Human Rights, Fifty-ninth session, 15 June 2002, Footnote #4, p.23.
21. Bernard Avishai, *The Hebrew Republic*, Orlando, FL: Harcourt, Inc., 2008, p.54.
22. 'Court rejects group appeal to be declared "Israeli" in IDs', *Israel National News*, 15 July 2008; see also 'So

this Jew, Arab, Georgian and Samaritan go to court ...', *Ha'aretz*, 28 December 2003.

23. 'Israel extends ban on immigration through marriage', *AFP*, 2 Jan 2011.
24. www.old-adalah.org/eng/intl04/eurcomm-pr.pdf (last accessed 21 June 2011).
25. 'Extension to citizenship law's validity is latest in a series of Israeli policies of racial separation based on national belonging', *Adalah*, 7 July 2008.
26. 'Supreme court to decide soon on whether the citizenship law, which discriminates on the basis of nationality and violates the right to family life, is compatible with Israel's basic laws', *Adalah*, 16 March 2009.
27. Meron Rapoport, 'Law that divides husband and wife', *Le Monde Diplomatique*, February 2004.
28. 'Legislation seeks to hinder citizenship for Palestinians, non-Jews', *Ha'aretz*, 5 April 2005.
29. Ibid.
30. 'Government plans tough new policy on citizenship, immigration', *Ha'aretz*, 11 May 2005.
31. 'Loyalty oath to "Jewish state" set to be approved', *Jerusalem Post*, 6 October 2010.
32. United Nations General Assembly Resolution 181, November 29, 1947, www.yale.edu/lawweb/avalon/un/res181.htm (last accessed 21 June 2011).
33. Knesset website, United Nations General Assembly Resolution 181, November 29, 1947, www.yale.edu/lawweb/avalon/un/res181.htm (last accessed 21 June 2011).
34. Hussein Abu Hussein and Fiona McKay, *Access Denied*, London: Zed Books, 2003, p.23.
35. Ibid. pp.23–24.
36. Kretzmer, *The Legal Status of the Arabs in Israel*, p.7.
37. Ibid. p.11.
38. Ibid. p.28.
39. 'Israel extends 63-year state of emergency – over ice cream and show tickets', *Ha'aretz*, 24 May 2011.
40. 'A state in emergency', *Ha'aretz*, 19 June 2005.

41. Ibid.
42. US State Department, 'International Religious Freedom Report 2010', www.state.gov/g/drl/rls/irf/2010/148825.htm (last accessed 21 June 2011).
43. Kretzmer, *The Legal Status of the Arabs in Israel*, p.8.
44. Ari Shavit, 'Formative words', *Ha'aretz*, 9 May 2011.
45. Tekiner, 'The "Who is a Jew" Controversy in Israel: A Produce of Political Zionism', p.71.
46. Davis, *Apartheid Israel*, p.30.
47. John Quigley, *Palestine and Israel: A Challenge to Justice*, Durham, NC: Duke University Press, 2000, p.118.
48. 'Birth of a nation', *Ha'aretz*, 30 October 2002.
49. Avishai, *The Hebrew Republic*, p.53.
50. 'NGOs to petition against "racist laws"', *Jerusalem Post*, 24 March 2011.
51. Yiftachel, *Ethnocracy*, p.93.
52. 'Safed rabbis urge Jews to refrain from renting apartments to Arabs', *Ha'aretz*, 20 October 2010; 'Shas spiritual leader may back ban on renting to Arabs', *Ha'aretz*, 29 October 2010.
53. 'Lands conference awards Safed rabbi who said Jews shouldn't rent to non-Jews', *Ha'aretz*, 28 April 2011.
54. Lev Luis Grinberg, 'Occupation laws in Israel?' *Ha'aretz*, translated and published on *Tikkun* website, 7 January 2011, www.tikkun.org/article.php/Jan72011Grinberg (last accessed 21 June 2011).
55. Yiftachel, *Ethnocracy*, p.3.
56. Ibid. p.16.
57. Jonathan Cook, *Disappearing Palestine: Israel's Experiments in Human Despair*, London: Zed Books, 2008, p.38.
58. www.mfa.gov.il/MFA/Peace+Process/Key+Speeches/PM+Sharon+addresses+the+UN+General+Assembly+15-Sep-2005.htm (last accessed 21 June 2011).
59. 'The new pioneers', *Jerusalem Post*, 5 February 2010.
60. Gershon Shafir and Yoav Peled, *Being Israeli: The Dynamics of Multiple Citizenship*, Cambridge: Cambridge University Press, 2002, p.125.

61. Lustick, *Arabs in the Jewish State*, p.65.
62. 'Equality and destruction', *Jerusalem Post*, 4 March 2007.
63. Meron Benvenisti, *Sacred Landscape*, Berkeley, CA: University of California Press, 2002, p.328.
64. 'The ghost town between Palestine's past and its future', *Independent*, 30 April 2011.
65. Gavison, 'The Jews' right to statehood: a defense', *Azure*.

CHAPTER 2. THE LAND REGIME

1. 'Israeli Arabs Grow Angry', *United Press International*, 26 March 1980.
2. Dan Rabinowitz and Khawla Abu-Baker, *Coffins on Our Shoulders: The Experience of the Palestinian Citizens of Israel*, Berkeley, CA: University of California Press, 2005, p.7.
3. Hussein and McKay, *Access Denied*, pp.289–90.
4. See, for example: 'Towns, villages and agricultural property were robbed without shame, and lawless individuals from the masses as well as the intelligentsia enriched themselves from occupied property', *Ha'aretz*, 26 July 1949, cited in Don Peretz, *Israel and the Palestine Arabs*, Washington DC: The Middle East Institute, 1958, p.154.
5. Benny Morris, *Israel's Border Wars, 1949–1956*, Oxford: Oxford University Press, 1997, p.118.
6. Benvenisti, *Sacred Landscape*, p.166.
7. Tom Segev, *1949: The First Israelis*, New York: Henry Holt, 1998, p.76.
8. Noga Kadman, 'How Nakba villages sunk into Israeli landscape', *+972blog*, 16 May 2011, http://972mag.com/nakbaerased (last accessed 21 June 2011); for more on the kibbutz movement and confiscation of Palestinian land see Asa Winstanley, 'The Receiving End of our Dreams', *New Left Project*, 7 October 2010, www.newleftproject.org/index.php/site/article_comments/the_receiving_end_of_our_dreams (last accessed 23 June 2011).

9. Benny Morris, *The Birth of the Palestinian Refugee Problem Revisited*, Cambridge: Cambridge University Press, 2004, p.369.
10. Benvenisti, *Sacred Landscape*, p.164.
11. Ibid. p.182.
12. Peretz, *Israel and the Palestine Arabs*, p.143.
13. Ibid. p.143.
14. Ibid. p.146.
15. Holzman-Gazit, *Land Expropriation in Israel*, p.104.
16. Segev, *1949: The First Israelis*, p.81.
17. Peretz, *Israel and the Palestine Arabs*, p.142.
18. Kretzmer, *The Legal Status of the Arabs in Israel*, p.56.
19. David A. Wesley, *State Practices & Zionist Images: Shaping Economic Development in Arab Towns in Israel*, Oxford: Berghahn Books, 2009, p.110.
20. Peretz, *Israel and the Palestine Arabs*, p.162.
21. Kretzmer, *The Legal Status of the Arabs in Israel*, p.59.
22. Ibid., p.58; Wesley, *State Practices & Zionist Images*, p.109.
23. Wesley, *State Practices & Zionist Images*, p.110.
24. Hussein and McKay, *Access Denied*, p.81.
25. Davis, *Apartheid Israel*, p.178
26. Hussein and McKay, *Access Denied*, p.73.
27. Alexandre Kedar, 'The legal transformation of ethnic geography: Israeli law and the Palestinian landholder 1948–1967', *International Law and Politics*, Vol.33:923, 2001.
28. Ibid.
29. Ibid.
30. Lustick, *Arabs in the Jewish State*, p.176.
31. Oren Yiftachel, 'The internal frontier: territorial control and ethnic relations in Israel', in Oren Yiftachel and Avinoam Meir (eds), *Ethnic Frontiers and Peripheries: Landscapes of Development and Inequality in Israel*, Boulder, CO: Westview Press, 1998. pp.39–67.
32. Ibid., p.57.
33. Hussein and McKay, *Access Denied*, p.136.
34. Lustick, *Arabs in the Jewish State*, p.276, note 26.

35. Davis, *Apartheid Israel*, p.43.
36. Hussein and McKay, *Access Denied*, p.86.
37. 'New discriminatory laws and bills in Israel', *Adalah*, November 2010.
38. Emanuel Marx, *Bedouin of the Negev*, Manchester: Manchester University Press, 1967, pp.10, 12.
39. Monica Tarazi, 'Planning Apartheid in the Naqab', in *Middle East Report*, Winter 2009, Number 253, pp.32–36.
40. Marx, *Bedouin of the Negev*, p.14.
41. Yiftachel, *Ethnocracy*, p.197; Sabri Jiryis, *The Arabs in Israel*, New York: Monthly Review Press, 1976, p.122.
42. Safa Abu-Rabia, 'Memory, belonging and resistance: the struggle over place among the Bedouin-Arabs of the Naqab/Negev', in Tovi Fenster and Haim Yacobi (eds), *Remembering, Forgetting and City Builders*, Farnham: Ashgate, 2010, pp.65–84 (71).
43. Ibid. p.71.
44. Yiftachel, *Ethnocracy*, p.198.
45. Ibid., p.193.
46. Tarazi, 'Planning Apartheid in the Naqab', p.33.
47. Ibid. p.33.
48. 'Evicting the Bedouins', *Time*, 6 August 1979.
49. Alon Tal, *Pollution in a promised land: an environmental history of Israel*, Berkeley, CA: University of California Press, 2002, p.347.
50. *Jerusalem Post*, 8 August 1977, cited in Lustick, *Arabs in the Jewish State*, p.258.
51. Rebecca Manski, 'Self-distraction from the environmental crisis: Bedouin vilified among top 10 environmental hazards in Israel', *News From Within*, February 2006.
52. 'Israelis chase Bedouins from desert', *Associated Press*, 29 December 1981.
53. 'Netanyahu's office promoting plan to relocate 30,000 Bedouin', *Ha'aretz*, 2 June 2011.
54. 'Netanyahu's controversial plan to divide the Negev', *Ynetnews.com*, 29 May 2011; 'Vote on Bedouin housing postponed', *Ynetnews.com*, 1 June 2011.

55. 'Jewish town to be built on Bedouin land under Negev relocation plan', *Ha'aretz*, 3 June 2011.
56. 'Bedouins slated to get ownership of Negev lands', *Ynetnews.com*, 10 March 2011.
57. Hillel Cohen, 'The State of Israel *versus* the Palestinian internal refugees', in Nur Masalha, (ed.) *Catastrophe Remembered: Palestine, Israel and the Internal Refugees*, London: Zed Books, 2005, pp.56–72 (63).
58. Nur Masalha, 'Present absentees and indigenous resistance', in Nur Masalha, (ed.) *Catastrophe Remembered: Palestine, Israel and the Internal Refugees*, London: Zed Books, 2005, pp.23–55 (36).
59. Ibid., p.37.
60. 'Cabinet rejects Biram and Ikrit villagers plea to return', *Ha'aretz*, 10 October 2001.
61. 'High Court rejects the right of Ikrit refugees to return home', *Ha'aretz*, 26 July 2003.
62. 'Raising a third generation on the uprooting of Ikrit', *Ha'aretz*, 29 March 2005.
63. Isabelle Humphries, 'Israeli citizens?: Palestinian displacement inside the Green Line', *Labour Representation Committee*, March 2009.
64. Hussein and McKay, *Access Denied*, p.3.
65. 'Plan to keep Israeli Arabs off some land is backed', *New York Times*, 9 July 2002.
66. Benvenisti, *Sacred Landscape*, p.177.
67. Hussein and McKay, *Access Denied*, p.172.
68. Ibid., pp.151–3.
69. JNF website, http://support.jnf.org/site/PageServer?pagename=Essence_of_Life (last accessed 21 June 2011).
70. Davis, *Apartheid Israel*, p.57.
71. 'Land controlled by Jewish National Fund for Jews only', *Adalah*, 29 July 2007.
72. Hussein and McKay, *Access Denied*, p.189.
73. Kretzmer, *The Legal Status of the Arabs in Israel*, p.94.
74. Ibid., p.97.
75. Ibid., p.97.

76. 'Jewish Agency readies plan to foster a "Zionist majority"', *Ha'aretz*, 28 October 2002.
77. Ben White, 'Real reform in Israel is a distant prospect', *Guardian – Comment is free*, 27 September 2009.
78. 'After years of planning, PM announces wide land reforms', *Jerusalem Post*, 19 May 2011; Amotz Asa-El, 'Netanyahu's other crisis', *MarketWatch*, 20 May 2011.
79. 'New Discriminatory Laws and Bills in Israel', *Adalah*.
80. 'JNF's strange place in the sun', *Globes*, 28 March 2010.
81. 'The New Israeli Land Reform', *Adalah's Newsletter*, Volume 63, August 2009.
82. JNF website, www.jnf.org/about-jnf/news/understanding_land_swap.html (last accessed 21 June 2011).
83. 'New discriminatory laws and bills in Israel', *Adalah*.
84. 'Foreign nationals limited from purchasing ownership of land', *Jerusalem Post*, 29 March 2011.
85. 'Bill approved forbidding sale of land to foreigners', *Jerusalem Post*, 17 March 2011.
86. 'UN CESCR Information Sheet No.3: Land and Housing Rights – Palestinian Citizens of Israel', *Adalah*, 2003.
87. Ibid.; Hussein and McKay, *Access Denied*, p.8.
88. Thanks to Adalah attorney Suhad Bishara for this data, referencing the Statistical Abstract of Israel 2010.
89. 'UN CESCR Information Sheet No.3: Land and Housing Rights – Palestinian Citizens of Israel', *Adalah*, 2003.
90. Wesley, *State Practices & Zionist Images*, p.130.
91. Michal Schwartz, 'Still Landless in Zion', *Challenge*, Issue 90, March/April 2005.
92. Hussein and McKay, *Access Denied*, p.219.
93. 'Israeli Arabs have no choice but to build illegally', *Ha'aretz*, 29 July 2010.
94. Wesley, *State Practices & Zionist Images*, p.35.
95. 'Off the Map', *Human Rights Watch*, 2008.
96. Ibid.
97. Ibid.
98. Yiftachel, 'The Internal Frontier', p.54.
99. Ibid., p.60.

100. 'Equality and Integration of the Arab Citizens in the Misgav Region', *Sikkuy-Misgav*, September 2001.
101. 'UN CESCR Information Sheet No.3: Land and Housing Rights – Palestinian Citizens of Israel', *Adalah*, 2003.
102. Hussein and McKay, *Access Denied*, p.228.
103. 'Stop creating forests that are destroying Bedouin lives', *Amnesty International*, 11 April 2011.
104. Hussein and McKay, *Access Denied*, p.259.
105. 'Getting onto the map', *Jerusalem Post*, 5 November 2010.
106. Hussein and McKay, *Access Denied*, p.268.
107. Noga Malkin, 'Erasing links to the land in the Negev', *Foreign Policy*, 11 March, 2011.
108. 'Arab Bedouin leader protesting home demolitions released from detention', *Adalah*, 22 February 2011.
109. 'Peres calls for equality at Iftar dinner', *Jerusalem Post*, 17 August 2010.
110. Noga Malkin, 'Erasing links to the land in the Negev'.
111. Ben White, 'Israel's "law of citizenship" will have dire consequences', *New Statesman* online, 19 October 2010.
112. 'Israel: grant status long denied to Arab village in central Israel', *Human Rights Watch*, 8 October 2010.
113. Ibid.
114. Ibid.
115. Ben White, 'Throughout Israel, Palestinians are being suffocated' *New Statesman* online, 5 August 2010.
116. 'Israel: Grant Status Long Denied to Arab Village in Central Israel', *Human Rights Watch*.
117. Hussein and McKay, *Access Denied*, p.47.
118. Ibid., p.271.
119. Oren Yiftachel, '"Creeping apartheid" in Israel-Palestine', in *Middle East Report*, Winter 2009, Number 253.
120. 'The equality index of Jewish and Arab citizens in Israel', *Sikkuy*, 2009.
121. 'During 2005–2009 the Israel Land Administration (ILA) provided the Arabic community with only 21% of its needed land for housing purposes', *The Arab Centre for Alternative Planning*, 18 March 2010.

122. Hussein and McKay, *Access Denied*, p.235.
123. '165 Buildings Owned by Arabs Were Demolished in 2009', *The Arab Centre for Alternative Planning*, 21 January 2010.
124. *Negev Coexistence Forum For Civil Equality*, Newsletter, May 2011.
125. 'Israel to triple demolition rate for illegal Bedouin construction', *Ha'aretz*, 18 February 2010.
126. 'Lod protesters call for housing dispute to be resolved', *Jerusalem Post*, 4 March 2011.
127. 'Israel: stop discriminatory home demolitions', *Human Rights Watch*, 8 March 2011.
128. *Adalah's Newsletter*, Volume 42, November 2007, www.adalah.org/newsletter/eng/nov07/8.php (last accessed 21 June 2011); 'There are now 695 communities in Israel where Arab citizens of the state are forbidden to live', *Adalah*, 4 November 2010.
129. 'Off the Map', *Human Rights Watch*.
130. Avishai, *The Hebrew Republic*, p.33.
131. 'Jewish town won't let Arab build home on his own land', *Ha'aretz*, 14 December 2009.
132. 'Plan to keep Israeli Arabs off some land is backed', *New York Times*, 9 July 2002.
133. 'Israel Backs Off Bill to Curb Arab Home Buying', *New York Times*, 15 July 2002.
134. 'Knesset approves preliminary vote on communities' admission policies', *Ynetnews.com*, 9 December 2009.
135. Ibid.; 'Knesset Panel Okays Bill Aimed at Pro-Arab Court Ruling', *Israel National News*, 7 December 2009.
136. 'MK Tibi: Arabs born here, some Jews fascists', *Ynetnews.com*, 22 December 2009.
137. 'Knesset panel approves controversial bill allowing towns to reject residents', *Ha'aretz*, 27 January 2010.
138. 'Can't we all just get along – separately?' *Ha'aretz*, 24 February 2011.
139. 'Israel: new laws marginalize Palestinian Arab citizens', *Human Rights Watch*, 30 March 2011; 'Plenum holds vote on controversial bills', *Jerusalem Post*, 23 March

2011; 'There are now 695 communities in Israel where Arab citizens of the state are forbidden to live', *Adalah*. At the time of writing, human rights groups have lodged petitions against the law with the Supreme Court, and the case is ongoing.

CHAPTER 3. JUDAISATION AND THE DEMOGRAPHIC THREAT

1. Hillel Cohen, *Good Arabs*, Berkeley, CA: University of California Press, 2010, p.97.
2. Haim Yacobi, *The Jewish-Arab City: Spatio-politics in a Mixed Community*, Abingdon: Routledge, 2009, p.9.
3. Gideon Levy, 'The threat of the "demographic threat"', *Ha'aretz*, 22 July 2007.
4. 'The Herzliya Conference on the balance of national strength and security in Israel', *Journal of Palestine Studies*, XXXI, no. 1, 2001, pp.50–61.
5. 'Benizri reconvenes long-dormant council on demography today', *Ha'aretz*, 3 September 2002.
6. 'Birth of a nation', *Ha'aretz*, 30 October 2002.
7. 'Israel must remain Jewish', *Ynetnews.com*, 4 April 2005.
8. 'Netanyahu: Israel's Arabs are the real demographic threat', *Ha'aretz*, 18 December 2003.
9. 'Jews, Arabs Debate Internal Arab Threat and 2-State Solution', *Israel National News*, 17 May 2010.
10. 'Jerusalem Mayor: Arab population in capital a strategic threat', *Jerusalem Post*, 13 January 2010; 'Report: Jerusalem's Arab population growing faster than its Jews', *Associated Press*, 10 June 1998.
11. 'Yishai: Let's restrict citizenship for Arab spouses', *Ha'aretz*, 9 January 2002.
12. 'Israeli Arab birthrate drops, first time in years', *Ha'aretz*, 24 January 2005.
13. 'A more effective birth control', *Ha'aretz*, 1 February 2005.

14. Brig. Gen. (res.) Eival Gilady, 'The Galilee as a challenge and national priority', Herzliya Conference, 23 January 2006.
15. 'Danny Ayalon: Galilee Arabs are secessionist threat', *Ha'aretz*, 2 September 2008.
16. 'Israel: Halt Demolitions of Bedouin Homes in Negev', *Human Rights Watch*, 1 August 2010.
17. Jonathan Cook, *Blood and Religion*, London: Pluto Press, 2006, p.109.
18. 'Boim: Is Palestinian terror caused by a genetic defect?' *Haa'retz*, 24 February 2004.
19. 'Housing Minister: spread of Arab population must be stopped', *Ha'aretz*, 2 July 2009.
20. Tawfiq S. Rangwala, 'Inadequate housing, Israel, and the Bedouin of the Negev', *Osgoode Hall Law Journal*, Volume 42, Number 3, 2004.
21. 'W. Bank rabbi: pay Beduin to move to Libya, Saudi Arabia', *Jerusalem Post*, 26 April 2011.
22. 'Lapid lambastes "barbaric" settlers', *Ha'aretz*, 19 December 2003.
23. 'One gunman, many to blame', *Arab Association for Human Rights*, October 2005.
24. *+972blog*, http://972mag.com/israel-builds-town-to-ensure-the-arabs-wont-rear-their-heads (last accessed 22 June 2011).
25. For example, leading activists in the extreme rightist group Lehava, known for initiatives like 'providing special certificates' for businesses that employ 'only Jews', are closely linked to another, state-funded NGO. 'Rightists seek to reward firms that don't hire gentiles', *Ha'aretz*, 2 February 2011; 'A strange kind of mercy', *Ha'aretz*, 27 May 2011.
26. 'Ashkelon rally targets Arabs who "seduce girls"', *Ynetnews.com*, 1 February 2011.
27. *Coteret* blog, http://coteret.com/2010/02/24/tel-aviv-presents-municipal-program-to-prevent-arab-boys-from-dating-jewish-girls (last accessed 22 June 2011).

28. 'MKs told more education is needed to combat intermarriage', *Jerusalem Post*, 11 February 2011.
29. 'Marriage to an Arab is national treason', *Ynetnews.com*, 27 March 2007.
30. The Guttman Center's Democracy Index for 2007.
31. The Guttman Center's Democracy Index for 2006.
32. 'Poll: 36% of Jews want to revoke Arabs' voting rights', *Ynetnews.com*, 15 October 2010.
33. David A. Wesley, *State Practices & Zionist Images: Shaping Economic Development in Arab Towns in Israel*, Oxford: Berghahn Books, 2009, p.120.
34. 'Israel: Pogrom at Home?' *Time*, 11 October 1976.
35. Rhoda Ann Kanaaneh, *Birthing the nation: strategies of Palestinian women in Israel*, Berkeley, CA: University of California Press, 2002, p.53.
36. 'Israel: Pogrom at Home?' *Time*.
37. Ibid. Ian Lustick, *Arabs in the Jewish State*, Austin, TX: University of Texas Press, 1980, p.68.
38. Lustick, *Arabs in the Jewish State*, p.333.
39. *Promised Land* blog, www.promisedlandblog.com/?p=2246 (last accessed 22 June 2011).
40. Geremy Forman, 'Reapproaching the borders of Nazareth (1948–1956), in Sandra Sufian and Mark LeVine (eds), *Reapproaching borders: new perspectives on the study of Israel-Palestine*, Lanham, MD: Rowman & Littlefield Publishers, 2007, pp.67–94 (82).
41. Ibid., p.84.
42. Dan Rabinowitz, 'The Frontiers of Urban Mix: Palestinians, Israelis, and Settlement Space', in Oren Yiftachel and Avinoam Meir (eds), *Ethnic Frontiers and Peripheries: Landscapes of Development and Inequality in Israel,* Boulder, CO: Westview Press, 1998, pp.69–85 (71).
43. Wesley, *State Practices and Zionist Images*, p.29.
44. Laurie King-Irani, 'A nixed, not mixed, city: mapping obstacles to democracy in the Nazareth/Natzerat Illit conurbation', in Daniel Monterescu and Dan Rabinowitz (eds), *Mixed Towns, Trapped Communities: Historical*

Narratives, Spatial Dynamics, Gender Relations and Cultural Encounters in Palestinian-Israeli Towns, Aldershot: Ashgate, 2007, pp.179–200 (180).

45. 'Natzrat Illit to build Chareidi neighborhood to counter Arabs moving in', *Matzav.com*, 25 June 2009.
46. 'Rabbi: Nazareth Illit must be Judaized', *Ynetnews.com*, 27 July 2009.
47. 'One city, two peoples', *Ha'aretz*, 8 August 2008.
48. 'Nazareth Illit: Mayor Brings Jews Back in Droves', *Israel National News*, 11 August 2010.
49. *+972blog*, http://972mag.com/how-the-mayor-of-a-nazareth-suburb-stole-christmas-2 (last accessed 22 June 2011).
50. 'More Israeli Arabs would have been killed in 2000 riots had I been in charge', *Ha'aretz*, 5 June 2011.
51. Wesley, *State Practices and Zionist Images*, p.28; Yifat Holzman-Gazit, *Land Expropriation in Israel: Law, Culture and Society*, Aldershot: Ashgate, 2007, p.140.
52. Jewish Agency for Israel website, www.jewishagency.org/JewishAgency/English/Jewish+Education/Compelling+Content/Eye+on+Israel/hityashvut/Hityashvut.htm (last accessed 22 June 2011).
53. Wesley, *State Practices and Zionist Images*, p.31; Oren Yiftachel, 'The Internal Frontier: Territorial Control and Ethnic Relations in Israel', in Oren Yiftachel and Avinoam Meir (eds), *Ethnic Frontiers and Peripheries: Landscapes of Development and Inequality in Israel*, Boulder, CO: Westview Press, 1998, pp.39–67 (58).
54. 'The view from the hilltops', *Ha'aretz*, 14 October 2010.
55. Howard M. Sachar, *A History of Israel*, New York: Knopf, 1996, p.842; 'Settle the Hilltops – or not', *Ha'aretz*, 23 February 2009.
56. 'Unacceptable Norms', *Ha'aretz*, 26 September 2004.
57. 'Land struggle of Israel's Bedouin', *BBC Newsnight*, 27 February 2007.
58. 'Off the Map', *Human Rights Watch*, 2008.
59. 'Beduin in Limbo', *Jerusalem Post*, 24 December 2007.

60. 'PMO Issues Rush Order for 30 New Towns in Negev, Galilee', *Ha'aretz*, 20 July 2003.
61. Hana Hamdan, 'The Policy of Settlement and "Spatial Judaization" in the Naqab', *Adalah's Newsletter*, Volume 11, March 2005.
62. Ibid.
63. Israeli Ministry of Foreign Affairs website, www.mfa.gov.il/MFA/Peace+Process/Reference+Documents/Exchange+of+letters+Sharon-Bush+14-Apr-2004.htm (last accessed 22 June 2011).
64. 'Pro-Israel Lobby Girding For Tough Battle on Aid', *Forward*, 15 April 2005.
65. 'KKL-JNF Embraces the Negev, its People and the Desert Environment', www.kkl.org.il/infogeneral/World Leadership Conference/Materials/KKL_NEGEV_LOW-embraces0304.pdf (last accessed 22 June 2011).
66. Uriel Heilman, 'The Negev's 21st Century Pioneers', *B'nai B'rith Magazine*, Winter 2008–09, www.urielheilman.com/0101negev.html (last accessed 22 June 2011).
67. Oren Yiftachel, *Ethnocracy: Land and Identity Politics in Israel/Palestine*, Philadellphia: University of Pennsylvania Press, 2006, p.3.
68. JNF website, http://support.jnf.org/site/PageServer?pagename=PR_Herzliya_Conf_2004 (last accessed 22 June 2011).
69. 'Demographic War: 'Suicidal Democracy' Lets Bedouin Conquer Negev', *Israel National News*, 26 September 2009.
70. Dr Thabet Abu-Ras, 'Land Disputes in Israel: The Case of the Bedouin of the Naqab', *Adalah's Newsletter*, Volume 24, April 2006.
71. 'Jewish Communities Planned to "Block Bedouin Expansion"', *Ha'aretz*, 5 June 2004.
72. Lustick, *Arabs in the Jewish State*, p.103.
73. 'Jewish Agency Readies Plan to Foster a "Zionist Majority"', *Ha'aretz*, 28 October 2002.
74. Jewish Agency for Israel website, www.jafi.org.il/press/2003/feb/feb19.htm (last accessed 22 June 2011).

75. Hussein Abu Hussein and Fiona McKay, *Access Denied*, London: Zed Books, 2003, pp.21–22.
76. 'Realizing Visions in the Negev JNF America – Missions Visit', *Jerusalem Post*, 12 January 2010.
77. 'Restorative for a Shrinking Israel?' the *Jerusalem Post*, 22 November 2005.
78. 'Pro-Negev Umbrella Council to be Created in Effort to Form Effective Lobby', *Jerusalem Post*, 23 December 2009.
79. 'Israeli Supreme Court Upholds Planning Authority Decision to Establish Individual Settlements in the Naqab as part of its "Wine Path Plan" Despite Discrimination against Arab Bedouin Unrecognized Villages', *Adalah*, 28 June 2010.
80. Wesley, *State Practices and Zionist Images*, p.39.
81. Hana Hamdan, 'Individual Settlement in the Naqab: The Exclusion of the Arab Minority', *Adalah's Newsletter*, Volume 10, February 2005.
82. *Adalah*, 28 June 2010.
83. 'Fencing out the Bedouin', *Ha'aretz*, 1 June 2003; *Adalah*, 28 June 2010.
84. 'New Discriminatory Laws and Bills in Israel', *Adalah*, November 2010.
85. Neve Gordon, 'Bitter Wine for Israel's Bedouins', *The Nation*, 5 June 2006.
86. 'People and Politics / Come Settle in the Negev', *Ha'aretz*, 1 June 2004.
87. 'Government Plans Land Giveaway to Combat Troops', *Ha'aretz*, 25 January 2010.
88. Prime Minister's Office website, www.pmo.gov.il/PMOEng/Communication/Spokesman/2010/06/spokestudy060610.htm (Last accessed 22 June 2011).
89. '"This is My State. I'm an Israeli Patriot": An Interview with Druze MK Ayoub Kara', *The Jewish Press*, 18 August 2010.
90. Kanaaneh, *Birthing the Nation*, p.52.
91. 'Interview: Homing in on Next Pullback', *Jerusalem Post*, 8 June 2006.

92. 'Cabinet Okays New National Priority Map Including Settlements', *Ha'aretz*, 14 December 2009; 'Jewish population in Galilee declining', *Ynetnews.com*, 12 December 2007.
93. 'Shalom aims to attract 600,000 to periphery by 2020', *Jerusalem Post*, 15 September 2009; 'Ayalon: Strengthen Jewish Periphery or Risk Arab Autonomy Try', *Israel National News*, 22 December 2009.
94. Holzman-Gazit, *Land Expropriation in Israel*, pp.139, 140.
95. 'State Lands Being Commandeered by Arabs', *Ynetnews.com*, 21 August 2009.
96. Yacobi, *The Jewish-Arab City*, p.9.

CHAPTER 4. SYSTEMATIC DISCRIMINATION

1. David A. Wesley, *State Practices & Zionist Images: Shaping Economic Development in Arab Towns in Israel*, Oxford: Berghahn Books, 2009, p.68.
2. 'Decades of Tax Breaks for the Settler Population', *Ha'aretz*, 25 September 2003.
3. 'On the Israeli Government's New Decision Classifying Communities as National Priority Areas', *Adalah*, February 2010.
4. 'Jews, Arabs React to Jewish Preference Ruling', *Jerusalem Post*, 28 February 2006.
5. 'New Discriminatory Laws and Bills in Israel', *Adalah*, November 2010.
6. 'PM's Plan Would Put Some Settlements on Map of National Priority Communities', *Ha'aretz*, 10 December 2009.
7. 'On the Israeli Government's New Decision Classifying Communities as National Priority Areas', *Adalah*.
8. 'The Equality Index of Jewish and Arab Citizens in Israel', *Sikkuy*, 2009.
9. 'From Barriers to Opportunities: Mapping the barriers and policy recommendations for achieving equality

between the Arab and Jewish citizens of Israel', *Sikkuy*, August 2010.

10. Ibid.
11. 'UN CESCR Information Sheet No.3: Land and Housing Rights - Palestinian Citizens of Israel', *Adalah*, 2003.
12. 'Socio-Economic Fact Sheet', *Dirasat*, 2008; 'From Barriers to Opportunities', *Sikkuy*.
13. 'The Equality Index of Jewish and Arab Citizens in Israel', *Sikkuy*; 'Socio-Economic Fact Sheet', *Dirasat*.
14. 'Study: Arabs may be poorer, But Jews get More Welfare Funds', *Ha'aretz*, 28 March 2007.
15. *Mada al-Carmel*, Political Monitoring Report, Issue 10, 2010.
16. 'The Equality Index of Jewish and Arab Citizens in Israel', *Sikkuy*.
17. David Kretzmer, *The Legal Status of the Arabs in Israel*, Boulder, CO: Westview Press, 1990, p.118.
18. 'A Coexistence-Policy Imperative', *Ha'aretz*, 13 March 2009.
19. 'Citizens, But Not Equal', *Ha'aretz*, 16 August 2010.
20. 'The Sikkuy Report 2002–2003', *Sikkuy*, July 2003.
21. 'Current Knesset is the Most Racist in Israeli History', *Ha'aretz*, 21 March 2010.
22. Socio-Economic Fact Sheet', *Dirasat*; Jonathan Cook, 'No Arabic at McDonald's', *Al-Ahram Weekly*, 4–10 March 2004.
23. 'Intra-Arab Competition Wears on Arab-Owned Businesses', *Jerusalem Post*, 23 March 2011.
24. 'Survey: Managers Support Hiring Arabs, But Don't Act on it', *Ha'aretz*, 10 March 2010.
25. 'The Economy Wakes up to Israel's Arabs', *Ha'aretz*, 15 March 2010; 'State to Invest NIS 700m in Developing Arab Towns', *Ha'aretz*, 18 March 2010.
26. 'Israeli Arab sector has Fastest Growth Potential, says Bank Hapoalim CEO', *Ha'aretz*, 12 May 2011.
27. 'Hapoalim Chairman Sees Great Potential in Israeli-Arab sector', *Globes*, 11 May 2011; 'Israeli Arab sector has

fastest growth potential, says Bank Hapoalim CEO, *Ha'aretz*.

28. 'Stef Wertheimer's New Middle East', *Globes*, 5 January 2004.
29. Zama Coursen-Neff, 'Discrimination Against Palestinian Arab Children in the Israeli Educational System', *International Law and Politics*, 36, 2005, pp.749–816.
30. Daphna Golan-Agnon, 'Separate but Not Equal: Discrimination Against Palestinian Arab Students in Israel', *American Behavioral Scientist*, Volume 49 Number 8, April 2006.
31. 'The Equality Index of Jewish and Arab Citizens in Israel', *Sikkuy*.
32. 'Israel Aids its Needy Jewish Students more than Arab Counterparts', *Ha'aretz*, 12 August 2009.
33. 'Israel's Education Woes', *Ynetnews.com*, 21 September 2010.
34. Gershon Shafir and Yoav Peled, *Being Israeli: The Dynamics of Multiple Citizenship*, Cambridge: Cambridge University Press, 2002, p.121.
35. 'Second Class: Discrimination Against Palestinian Arab Children in Israel's Schools', *Human Rights Watch*, 2001.

CHAPTER 5. FRUSTRATING DEMOCRATIC CHANGE

1. Ian Lustick, *Arabs in the Jewish State*, Austin, TX: University of Texas Press, 1980, p.64.
2. Tom Segev, *1949: The First Israelis*, New York: Henry Holt, 1998, p.50.
3. Don Peretz, *Israel and the Palestine Arabs*, Washington DC: The Middle East Institute, 1958, p.95.
4. Segev, *1949*, p.67.
5. Lustick, *Arabs in the Jewish State*, p.68.
6. Peretz, *Israel and the Palestine Arabs*, p.96.
7. Benny Morris, *Israel's Border Wars, 1949–1956: Arab Infiltration, Israeli Retaliation, and the Countdown to*

the Suez War, Oxford: Oxford University Press, 1993, p.148; Ibid., p.170.

8. John Quigley, *The Case for Palestine: An International Law Perspective*, Durham, NC: Duke University Press, 2005, p.109.
9. Alina Korn, 'Crime and Law Enforcement in the Israeli Arab Population under the Military Government, 1948–1966', in Ilan S. Troen and Noah Lucas (eds), *Israel: The First Decade of Independence*, Albany, NY: State University of New York Press, 1991, pp.659–79 (660–61).
10. Korn, 'Crime and Law Enforcement in the Israeli Arab Population under the Military Government, 1948–1966', p.668; Peretz, *Israel and the Palestine Arabs*, p.97; Segev, *1949*, p.51.
11. Korn, 'Crime and Law Enforcement in the Israeli Arab Population under the Military Government, 1948–1966', p.668.
12. Lustick, *Arabs in the Jewish State*, p.125.
13. Ibid., p.125.
14. Ibid., p.67.
15. Ibid., p.66.
16. Cohen, *Good Arabs*, p.236; Lustick, *Arabs in the Jewish State*, p.192; Ibid. p.194.
17. Raja Shehadeh, 'Mahmoud Darwish', *BOMB*, 81/Fall 2002.
18. Haim Yacobi, 'Planning, Control and Spatial Protest: The Case of the Jewish-Arab Town of Lydd/Lod', in Daniel Monterescu and Dan Rabinowitz (eds), *Mixed Towns, Trapped Communities: Historical Narratives, Spatial Dynamics, Gender Relations and Cultural Encounters in Palestinian-Israeli Towns*, Aldershot: Ashgate, 2007, pp.135–55 (137–38).
19. Lustick, *Arabs in the Jewish State*, p.146.
20. Ibid., p.146.
21. Segev, *1949*, p.51.
22. Cohen, *Good Arabs*, p.2.
23. Ibid., p.235.

24. '60 Years Later, Spies' Lives Revealed', *Ynetnews.com*, 20 February 2011.
25. Peretz, *Israel and the Palestine Arabs*, p.129.
26. Ibid., p.129.
27. Cohen, *Good Arabs*, p.3.
28. Ibid., p.233.
29. Segev, *1949*, p.65.
30. Cohen, *Good Arabs*, p.3; Ibid., p.233.
31. Ibid., p.3.
32. Lustick, *Arabs in the Jewish State*, p.69.
33. Ibid., p.144.
34. Shany Payes, *Palestinian NGOs in Israel: the Politics of Civil Society*, London: I.B. Tauris, 2005, p.93.
35. Eric Rozenman, 'Israeli Arabs and the Future of the Jewish State', *Middle East Quarterly*, September 1999, pp.15–23.
36. 'Wikileaks Cable Dated 22 May 2008', *Guardian* website, 7 April 2011, www.guardian.co.uk/world/2011/apr/07/israel-gaza2 (last accessed 22 June 2011).
37. 'PMO to Balad: We will Thwart Anti-Israel Activity Even if Legal', *Ha'aretz*, 16 March 2007.
38. 'Shin Bet: Citizens subverting Israel key values to be probed', *Ha'aretz*, 20 May 2007.
39. Yitzhak Laor, 'Democracy for Jews only', *Ha'aretz*, 30 May 2007.
40. Ben White, 'Israel Subverts Human Rights for a Key Critic', LiberalConspiracy.org, May 29 2010, http://liberalconspiracy.org/2010/05/29/israel-subverts-human-rights-for-a-key-critic (last accessed 22 June 2011).
41. 'Palestinian Human Rights Activist Jailed in Israel', *Amnesty International*, 30 January 2011.
42. 'Knesset Passes "Nakba bill"', *Ynetnews.com*, 23 March 2011; 'Israel Passes Law Against Mourning its Existence', *Reuters*, 22 March 2011.
43. 'A Blow to Israeli Arabs and to Democracy', *Ha'aretz*, 22 March 2011.
44. 'Yisrael Beiteinu MK: Teaching the Nakba in Israel's schools is incitement', *Ha'aretz*, 24 March 2011.

45. 'Arab education officials: Israel must lift ban on teaching about Nakba', *Ha'aretz*, 28 April 2011; 'Unofficial Nakba study kit a hit with teachers', *Ha'aretz*, 14 June 2011.
46. Ben White, 'Marginalisation in Israel's Knesset', *New Statesman*, 24 March 2010.
47. Ben White, 'Targeting Israel's Palestinians', *Al Jazeera*, 23 June 2010.
48. 'Knesset C'tee: Strip MK Zouabi of Extra Rights', *Israel National News*, 7 June 2010.
49. 'Knesset Revokes Arab MK Zuabi's Privileges Over Gaza Flotilla', *Ha'aretz*, 13 July 2010; 'MK Zoabi Called "Embarrassment," "Traitor" in Stormy Session', *Israel National News*, 13 July 2010.
50. 'MK Levin: We Must Do Something About Arab Parties', *Israel National News*, 23 February 2010.
51. 'Amnesty Cites "Racism in Legal System" in Israel', *Ha'aretz*, 24 July 2001.
52. 'Judge: State Discriminating Between Jews, Arabs', *Ynetnews.com*, 11 November 2009.
53. Cohen, *Good Arabs*, p.136.
54. 'The Divided Loyalties of Israel's Arab Citizens', *Los Angeles Times*, 13 April 1976.
55. 'Summary of the Findings and Conclusions of Adalah's "The Accused" Report', *Adalah*, 2006.
56. 'Racism and the Administration of Justice', *Amnesty International*, 2001.
57. 'Mass arrests and police brutality' *Amnesty International*, November 2000.
58. 'Prohibited Protest: Law Enforcement Authorities Restrict the Freedom of Expression of Protestors against the Military Offensive in Gaza', *Adalah*, 2009.

CHAPTER 6. RETHINK TO REIMAGINE

1. Oren Yiftachel, "Creeping Apartheid' in Israel-Palestine', *Middle East Report*, Winter 2009, Number 253, pp.7–15, 37.

2. Ibid.
3. Ben White, 'Netanyahu: Erasing the Green Line', *Al Jazeera*, 27 April 2011.
4. Yehouda Shenhav, 'The Arabs of 1948: The Skeleton in the "Peace Process" Closet', *Jadal*, Issue no.10, June 2011.
5. Ben White, 'The Iconography of Revolt', *New Left Project* blog, 13 February 2011, www.newleftproject.org/index.php/site/blog_comments/the_iconography_of_revolt (last accessed 23 June 2011).
6. Ameer Makhoul, 'The Rebellions of our Peoples Make us Stronger', *The Electronic Intifada*, 17 June 2011.
7. Daniel Gavron, *The Other Side of Despair: Jews and Arabs in the Promised Land*, Lanham, MD: Rowman and Littlefield, 2004, p.229, cited in Ali Abunimah, *One Country*, New York: Henry Holt, 2006, p.172.
8. Nadim N. Rouhana, 'The Colonial Condition: Is Partition Possible in Palestine?' *Jadal*, Issue no. 10, June 2011.
9. See http://bdsmovement.net (last accessed 23 June 2011).
10. Amnon Raz-Krakotzkin, 'Separation and Bi-nationalism', *Jadal*, Issue no. 10, June 2011.
11. arenaofspeculation website, http://arenaofspeculation.org/2011/05/18/planning-al-awda-re-imagining-israel-palestine (last accessed, 23 June 2011).
12. Benny Morris, *Israel's Border Wars, 1949–1956*, Oxford: Oxford University Press, 1997, p.177.
13. Edward Said, *The Question of Palestine*, London: Vintage, 1992, p.244.

Select Bibliography

Abu Hussein, Hussein and Fiona McKay (2003) *Access Denied* (London: Zed Books).

Abu-Rabia, Safa (2010) 'Memory, Belonging and Resistance: The Struggle Over Place.

Among the Bedouin-Arabs of the Naqab/Negev', in Fenster, Tovi and Yacobi, Haim (eds) *Remembering, Forgetting and City Builders* (Farnham: Ashgate) pp.65–84.

Abu-Ras, Thabet (2006) 'Land Disputes in Israel: The Case of the Bedouin of the Naqab' (Adalah).

Abu-Saad, Ismael (2004) 'Education as a Tool of Expulsion from the Unrecognized Villages' (Adalah).

Abunimah, Ali (2006) *One Country* (New York: Henry Holt).

Adalah (2003) UN CESCR Information Sheet No.3: Land and Housing Rights – Palestinian Citizens of Israel.

—— (2009) 'Prohibited Protest: Law Enforcement Authorities Restrict the Freedom of Expression of Protestors against the Military Offensive in Gaza'.

—— (2010) 'On the Israeli Government's New Decision Classifying Communities as National Priority Areas'.

—— (2010a) 'New Discriminatory Laws and Bills in Israel'.

—— (2011) 'The Inequality Report: The Palestinian Arab Minority in Israel'.

Amnesty International (2001) 'Racism and the Administration of Justice'.

Arab Association for Human Rights (2005) 'On the Margins'.

—— (2005) 'One Gunman, Many to Blame'.

—— (2006) 'On the Margins'.

Arab Center for Alternative Planning (2007) 'Annual Narrative Report'.

Aruri, Naseer (ed.) (2001) *Palestinian Refugees: The Right of Return* (London: Pluto Press).

Baruch, Nili (2004) 'Spatial Inequality in the Allocation of Municipal Resources', *Adalah's Newsletter*, Vol. 8, December 2004.

Ben-Rafael, Eliezer and Peres, Yochanan Peres (2005) *Is Israel One? Religion, Nationalism, and Multiculturalism Confounded* (Leiden: Brill).

Benvenisti, Meron (2002) *Sacred Landscape* (Berkeley: University of California Press).

Bisharat, George (1994) 'Land, Law, and Legitimacy in Israel and the Occupied Territories', *The American University Law Review*, Vol. 43: 467.

Cohen, Erik (1989) 'Citizenship, Nationality and Religion in Israel and Thailand', in Kimmerling, Baruch (ed.), *The Israeli State and Society: Boundaries and Frontieres* (Albany, NY: State University of New York Press) pp.66–92.

Cohen, Hillel (2010) *Good Arabs* (Berkeley: University of California Press).

Cook, Jonathan (2006) *Blood and Religion* (London: Pluto Press).

—— (2008) *Disappearing Palestine: Israel's experiments in human despair* (London: Zed Books).

Davis, Uri (1990) *Israel: An Apartheid State* (London: Zed Books).

—— (2003) *Apartheid Israel* (London: Zed Books).

Dirasat (2008) 'Socio-Economic Fact Sheet'.

Forman, Geremy (2007) 'Reapproaching the borders of Nazareth (1948–1956), in Sufian, Sandra Marlene and LeVine, Mark (eds), *Reapproaching borders: new perspectives on the study of Israel-Palestine* (Lanham, MD: Rowman & Littlefield) pp.67–94.

Gavison, Ruth (2003) 'The Jews' Right to Statehood: A Defense', *Azure*, Summer 5763 / 2003, no. 15.

Hamdan, Hana (2005) 'The Policy of Settlement and "Spatial Judaization" in the Naqab', (Adalah).

—— (2005a) 'Individual Settlement in the Naqab: The Exclusion of the Arab Minority', (Adalah).

Hertzberg, Arthur (ed.) (1997) *The Zionist Idea* (Philadelphia: The Jewish Publication Society).

Holzman-Gazit, Yifat (2007) *Land expropriation in Israel: Law, Culture and Society* (Aldershot: Ashgate).

Human Rights Watch (2001) 'Second Class: Discrimination Against Palestinian Arab Children in Israel's Schools'.

—— (2008) 'Off the Map'.

Jabareen, Rafiq Yosef (2009) 'The Geo-Political and Spatial Implications of the New Israel Land Administration Law on the Palestinians', *Adalah's Newsletter*, Vol. 62, July 2009.

Jiryis, Sabri (1976) *The Arabs in Israel* (New York: Monthly Review Press).

Kanaaneh, Rhoda Ann (2002) *Birthing the Nation: Strategies of Palestinian Women in Israel* (Berkeley: University of California Press).

Kedar, Alexandre (2001) 'The Legal Transformation of Ethnic Geography: Israeli Law and the Palestinian Landholder 1948–1967', *International Law and Politics*, Vol. 33:923.

Kedar, Alexandre and Yiftachel, Oren (2006) 'Land Regime and Social Relations in Israel', in de Soto, Hernando and Cheneval, Francis (eds), *Swiss Human Rights Book Vol. 1* (Zurich: Rüffer & Rub).

Kimmerling, Baruch (1989) 'Boundaries and Frontiers of the Israeli Control System: Analytical Conclusions', in Kimmerling, Baruch (ed.), *The Israeli State and Society: Boundaries and Frontieres* (Albany, NY: State University of New York Press) pp.265–284.

King-Irani, Laurie (2007) 'A Nixed, not Mixed, City: Mapping Obstacles to Democracy in the Nazareth/Natzerat Illit Conurbation', in Daniel Monterescu and Dan Rabinowitz (eds), *Mixed Towns, Trapped Communities: Historical Narratives, Spatial Dynamics, Gender Relations and Cultural Encounters in Palestinian-Israeli Towns* (Aldershot: Ashgate) pp.179–200.

Kissak, Moshe (ed.) (1984) *Israeli Society and its Defense Establishment: The Social and Political Impact of a Protracted Violent Conflict* (London: Frank Cass).

Korn, Alina (1995) 'Crime and Law Enforcement in the Israeli Arab Population under the Military Government, 1948–1966', in Troen, Ilan S. and Lucas, Noah (eds), *Israel: The First*

Decade of Independence (Albany, NY: State University of New York Press) pp.659–679.

Kretzmer, David (1990) *The Legal Status of the Arabs in Israel* (Boulder, CO: Westview Press).

Lustick, Ian (1980) *Arabs in the Jewish State* (Austin, TX: University of Texas Press).

Mada al-Carmel (2011) 'Rethinking Partition of Palestine', *Jadal* Issue no.10, June 2011.

Marx, Emanuel (1967) *Bedouin of the Negev* (Manchester: Manchester University Press).

Masalha, Nur (ed.) (2005) *Catastrophe Remembered: Palestine, Israel and the Internal Refugees* (London: Zed Books).

Morris, Benny (1993) *Israel's Border Wars, 1949–1956: Arab Infiltration, Israeli Retaliation, and the Countdown to the Suez War* (Oxford: Oxford University Press).

Nathan, Susan (2005) *The Other Side of Israel* (London: HarperCollins).

Pappe, Ilan (1995) 'An Uneasy Coexistence: Arabs and Jews in the First Decade of Statehood', in Troen, Ilan S. and Lucas, Noah (eds), *Israel: The First Decade of Independence* (Albany, NY: State University of New York Press) pp.617–658.

—— (2011) *The Forgotten Palestinians: A History of the Palestinians in Israel* (New Haven, CT: Yale University Press).

Peretz, Don (1958) *Israel and the Palestine Arabs* (Washington DC: The Middle East Institute).

Quigley, John (1990) *Palestine and Israel: A Challenge to Justice* (Durham: Duke University Press).

Rabinowitz, Dan (1998) 'The Frontiers of Urban Mix: Palestinians, Israelis, and Settlement Space', in Oren Yiftachel and Avinoam Meir (eds), *Ethnic Frontiers and Peripheries: Landscapes of Development and Inequality in Israel* (Boulder, CO: Westview Press) pp.69–85.

—— (1997) *Overlooking Nazareth: The ethnography of exclusion in Galilee* (Cambridge: Cambridge University Press).

Rabinowitz, Dan and Abu-Baker, Khawla (2005) *Coffins on Our Shoulders: The Experience of the Palestinian Citizens of Israel* (Berkeley: University of California Press).

Rangwala, Tawfiq, S. (2004) 'Inadequate Housing, Israel, and the Bedouin of the Negev', *Osgoode Hall Law Journal*, Vol. 42, No. 3.

Rempel, Terry (ed.) (2009) *Rights in Principle – Rights in Practice: Revisiting the Role of International Law in Crafting Durable Solutions for Palestinian Refugees* (Bethlehem, Palestine: Badil Resouce Center).

Rosen-Zvi, Issachar (2004) *Taking Space Seriously: Law, Space, and Society in Contemporary Israel* (Aldershot: Ashgate).

Rouhana, Nadim N. and Sultany, Nimer (2003) 'Redrawing the Boundaries of Citizenship: Israel's New Hegemony', *Journal of Palestine Studies*, Vol. 33, No. 1.

Roy, Ananya and AlSayyad, Nezar (2003) *Urban Informality: Transnational Perspectives from the Middle East, Latin America, and South Asia* (Lanham, MD: Lexington).

Sa'di, Ahmad H. and Abu-Lughod, Lila (eds) (2007) *Nakba: Palestine, 1948, and the Claims of Memory* (New York: Columbia University Press).

Segev, Tom (1998) *1949: The First Israelis* (New York: Henry Holt).

Shafir, Gershon and Peled, Yoav (2002) *Being Israeli: The Dynamics of Multiple Citizenship* (Cambridge: Cambridge Univeristy Press).

Sikkuy (2005) 'Development of the Negev and Galilee, Policy Paper'.

—— (2009) 'The Equality Index of Jewish and Arab Citizens in Israel'.

—— (2010) 'From Barriers to Opportunities: Mapping the Barriers and Policy Recommendations for Achieving Equality Between the Arab and Jewish Citizens of Israel'.

Shoshan, Malkit (2010) *Atlas of the Conflict: Israel-Palestine* (Rotterdam: 010 Publishers).

Swirski, Shlomo (2007) *Current Plans for Developing the Negev: A Critical Perspective* (Adva Center).

Tal, Alon (2002) *Pollution in a Promised Land: An Environmental History of Israel* (Berkeley: University of California Press).

Tarazi, Monica (2009) 'Planning Apartheid in the Naqab', *Middle East Report*, Winter 2009, Number 253.

Tekiner, Roselle, Abed-Rabbo, Samir and Mezvinsky, Norton (eds) (1988), *Anti-Zionism: Analytical Reflections* (Brattleboro, VT: Amana Books).

'The Herzliya Conference on the balance of national strength and security in Israel' (2001) *Journal of Palestine Studies*, XXXI, no. 1, pp.50–61.

Tilley, Virginia (2005) *The One-State Solution* (Michigan: University of Michigan Press).

Wesley, David A. (2009) *State Practices & Zionist Images: Shaping Economic Development in Arab Towns in Israel* (Oxford: Berghahn Books).

White, Ben (2009) *Israeli Apartheid: A Beginner's Guide* (London: Pluto Press).

—— (2010) *Palestinians in Israel's 'democracy': The Judaization of the Galilee* (London: Middle East Monitor).

Yacobi, Haim (2007) 'Planning, Control and Spatial Protest: The Case of the Jewish-Arab Town of Lydd/Lod', in Daniel Monterescu and Dan Rabinowitz (eds), *Mixed Towns, Trapped Communities: Historical Narratives, Spatial Dynamics, Gender Relations and Cultural Encounters in Palestinian-Israeli Towns* (Aldershot: Ashgate) pp.135–155.

Yiftachel, Oren (1998) 'The Internal Frontier: Territorial Control and Ethnic Relations in Israel', in Oren Yiftachel and Avinoam Meir (eds), *Ethnic Frontiers and Peripheries: Landscapes of Development and Inequality in Israel* (Boulder, CO: Westview Press) pp.39–67.

—— (2006) *Ethnocracy: Land and Identity Politics in Israel/Palestine* (Philadelphia: University of Pennsylvania Press).

—— (2009) '"Creeping Apartheid" in Israel-Palestine', *Middle East Report*, Winter 2009, Number 253.

Zaher, Sawsan (2010) *The Prohibition on Teaching the Nakba in the Arab Education System in Israel* (Adalah).

Zureik, Elia (1979) *The Palestinians in Israel: A Study in Internal Colonialism* (London: Routledge and Kegan Paul).

Zureik, Elia, Lyon, David and Abu-Laban, Yasmeen (eds) (2010) *Surveillance and Control in Israel/Palestine: Population, Territory and Power* (London: Routledge).

Index

Made in the USA
Columbia, SC
31 December 2023

29705033R00088